The FORCE Companion

The FORCE Companion

Quick Tips and Tricks

Mike Mattesi
Swendly Benilia

CRC Press
Taylor & Francis Group
Boca Raton London New York

CRC Press is an imprint of the
Taylor & Francis Group, an **informa** business

CRC Press
Taylor & Francis Group
6000 Broken Sound Parkway NW, Suite 300
Boca Raton, FL 33487-2742

© 2019 by Taylor & Francis Group, LLC
CRC Press is an imprint of Taylor & Francis Group, an Informa business

No claim to original U.S. Government works

Printed on acid-free paper

International Standard Book Number-13: 978-1-138-34175-3 (Hardback)
978-1-138-34174-6 (Paperback)

Library of Congress Cataloging-in-Publication Data

Names: Mattesi, Michael D., author. | Benilia, Swendly, author.
Title: The Force companion : quick tips and tricks / Mike Mattesi and Swendly Benilia.
Description: Boca Raton : Taylor & Francis, a CRC title, part of the Taylor & Francis imprint,
a member of the Taylor & Francis Group, the academic division of T&F Informa, plc, 2019.
Identifiers: LCCN 2018051281| ISBN 9781138341746 (paperback :acid-free paper)
| ISBN 9781138341753 (hardback : acid-free paper)
Subjects: LCSH: Figure drawing--Technique. | Action in art. | Force and energy--Miscellanea.
Classification: LCC NC765 .M3773 2019 | DDC 741.2--dc23
LC record available at https://lccn.loc.gov/2018051281

Visit the Taylor & Francis Web site at
http://www.taylorandfrancis.com

and the CRC Press Web site at
http://www.crcpress.com

Contents

Preface

Dear FORCE Artist,

The most fulfilling moments in my teaching career are when my students accomplish their goals and design the life they want to live. Certain art students want to master the skills that I share and teach them as well. Teaching is a challenging career. You must have the ability to do that which you teach, analyze how and why you do it, define a clear system behind it and then have the ability to clearly explain it to others... while inspiring the student to believe in him or her self.

This book marks an important moment in the journey of the FORCE Drawing Method. The FORCE Companion: Quick Tips and Tricks is fully illustrated by someone other than me, one of my former students and now a FORCE instructor, Swendly Benilia.

Swendly learned what I know and developed his own voice, one where FORCE Shape drives his thinking process and thus creates clear and dynamic drawings full of FORCE. His own interest to help others on their FORCE journey has led us to the development of this book, a companion to the FORCE Drawing series.

This book exhibits drawings of FORCE along with short blurbs that share quick, insightful tips that will help you along your FORCE journey. So go use this book, flip through its many pages filled with hundreds of dynamic FORCE drawings and be inspired to learn and draw!

If you want to learn more about FORCE visit Swendly and me at DrawingFORCE.com

With much pride,

Mike Mattesi

Preface

*Inspiration is precious. I believe that if you can keep yourself inspired you'll be unstoppable! Thus the main intention of this companion book is to further inspire artists to see and draw the figure with **FORCE**. And what better way to achieve that than to feasting your eyes on hundreds of **FORCEFUL** figure drawings.*

*Most of the drawings in this book were created during my daily 1 hour warm-up sessions I do before work. As you will notice, athletes and dancers are my favorite subjects to draw. Their gestures are full of **FORCE** and drama, and their clearly defined muscles help me understand the figure's anatomy in the process.*

*When you look at the drawings in this book, keep in mind that what you see is essentially different applications of the **FORCE** Drawing fundamentals. A master at any craft is simply one who mastered the fundamentals.*

Swendly Benilia

Author

Swendly Benilia

I was born in Willemstad, Curaçao on December 1985. For as long as I can remember I've been creating characters in my mind. At first I wanted to become a comic book artist, but after discovering that there was someone drawing the environments and characters from all the cool video games I was playing, I decided to pursue a career in concept art.

In 2004 I moved to the Netherlands to study Industrial Design at The Hague University. After two years I realized it was not quite what I was looking for, so I switched to Game Design & Development at the Utrecht School of Art and Technology. I graduated in 2011 with a BA degree and a specialization in concept art for video games. Since drawing people and inventing characters is one of my greatest passions in life, I chose to further specialize in character design.

In my journey as an artist, I've learned that there are three major keys for success in any endeavor: wisdom, knowledge and understanding. So besides drawing and designing I make sure to keep learning and expand my knowledge on a daily basis, especially by reading good books.

My purpose in life is to be a person of value and make a significant contribution to the world by refining and serving my creative gift and inspiring others to do the same.

Chapter 1
FORCE Basics

DIRECTIONAL & APPLIED FORCE

*In FORCE Drawing we use line to communicate the idea of energy, or FORCE. A **Directional FORCE line** (1) shows the direction of the energy or its path. The line starts somewhere, does something, and goes somewhere. Think in this manner to avoid **scratchy lines** (2) or **hairy lines** (3).*

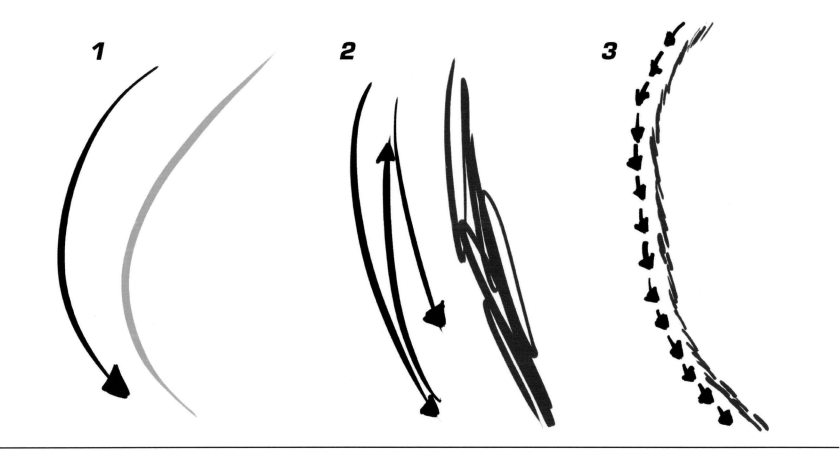

*Avoid **scratchy drawings**. Focus on the biggest ideas of the pose first. Look for the Directional FORCEs and be decisive with your marks.*

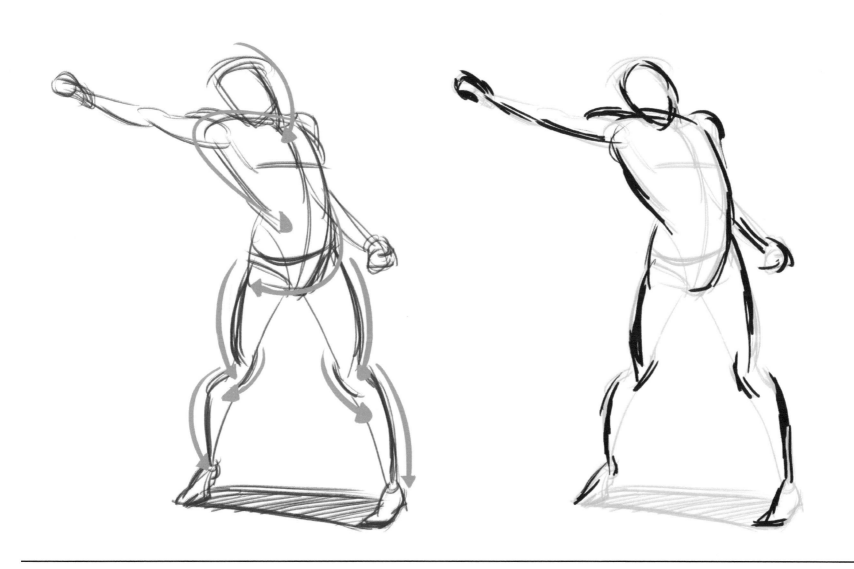

When a *Directional FORCE* applies itself to another *Directional FORCE* it becomes an **Applied FORCE**. The previous *Directional FORCE* determines how strong the **Applied FORCE** is.

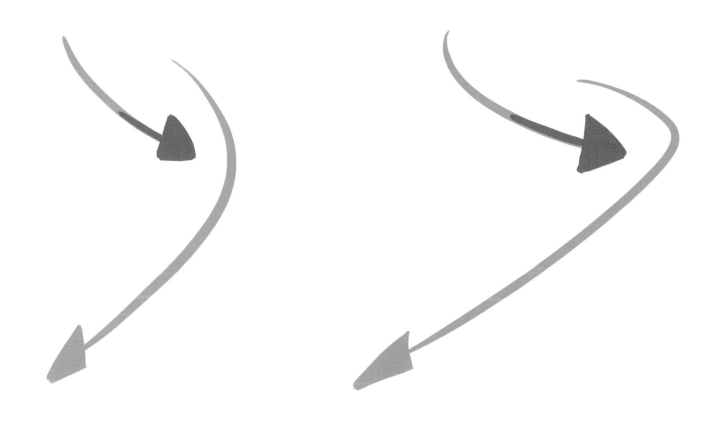

When you draw a *Directional FORCE*, also consider the amount of *Applied FORCE* on the curve. The more *Applied FORCE* the sharper the curve.

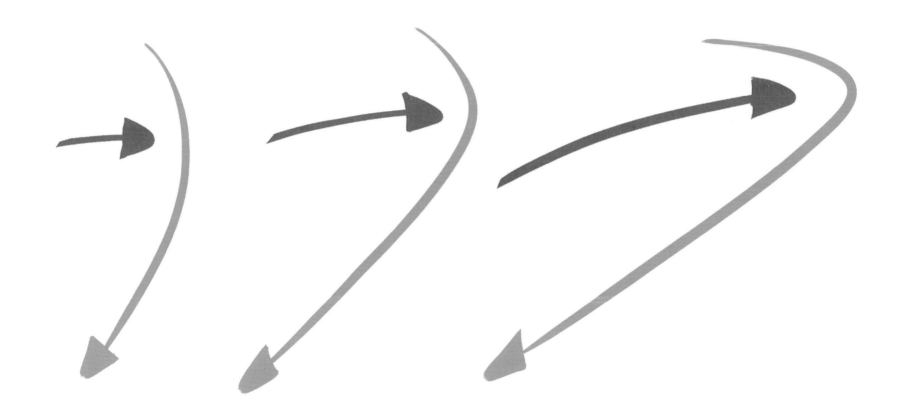

*Use darker Directional FORCE lines to show areas with the most **Applied FORCE**.*

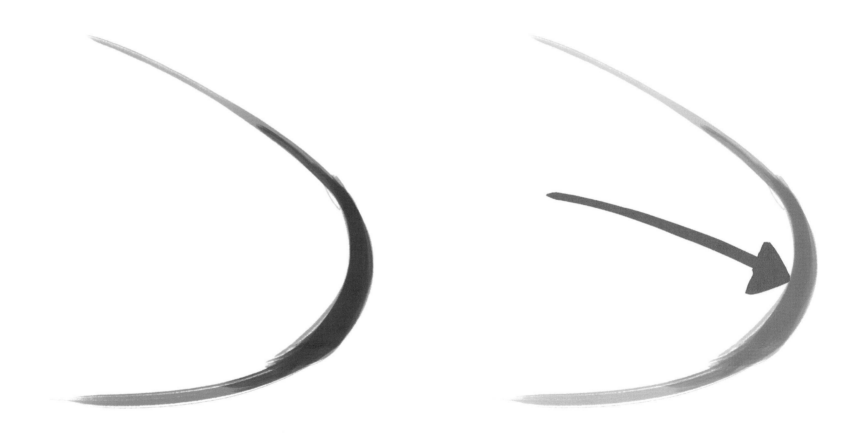

*Awareness of **Gravity** is an important aspect of FORCE Drawing. I draw darker **Directional FORCE** lines to show the weight on the athlete's shoulder area as **Gravity** pulls her down.*

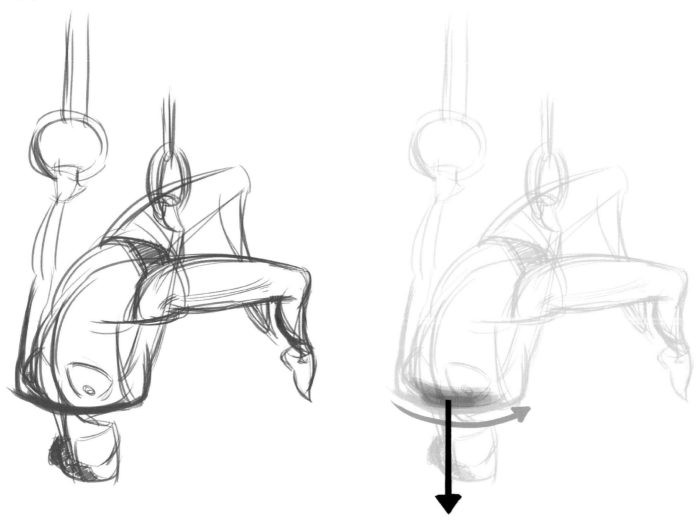

*I use **Applied FORCE** to draw the effort in this athlete's trapezius and upper back caused by the stiffness of her arms holding up the weight of her body. Watch how the **Applied FORCE** relates to the Directional FORCE.*

*I draw darker lines on this gymnast's back to show its **Applied FORCE** as she hangs from the bar. Observe how it relates to the back's Directional FORCE.*

I'm intrigued by this athlete's ability to support all his weight with his left arm during this action. I use darker Directional FORCE lines to show the Applied FORCE on his arm.

My main focus in this drawing is the **Applied FORCE** pushing out the dancer's rib cage. Notice how it affects the **Directional FORCE** of this area.

*This athlete's left leg supports all her weight as she lands. Look at all the **Applied FORCE**.*

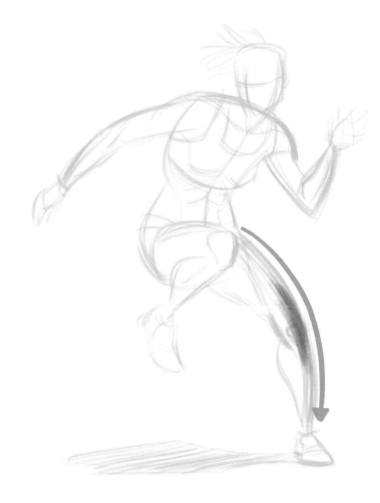

*I use darker lines to show the **Applied FORCEs** of this model's right leg as it supports most of his weight.*

This simple drawing presents a clear story. Notice the **Applied** and *Directional* *FORCEs* in the gymnast's arms as she supports her weight.

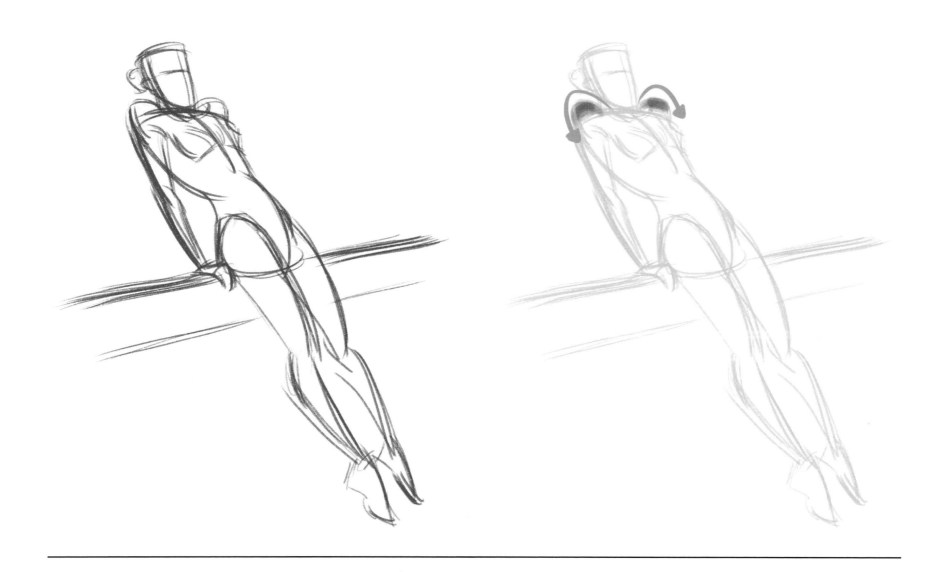

There are strong **Applied FORCEs** on this model's right leg as it supports all her weight. I use darker **Directional FORCE** lines to show this.

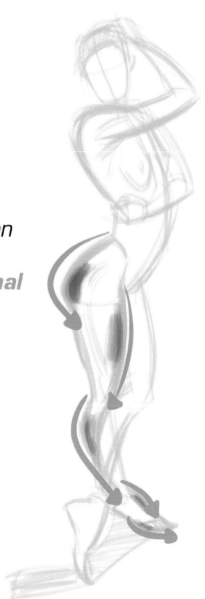

*I use darker lines and more definition in this dancer's right leg to show all the effort it puts into supporting her weight. Notice the areas of **Applied FORCE**.*

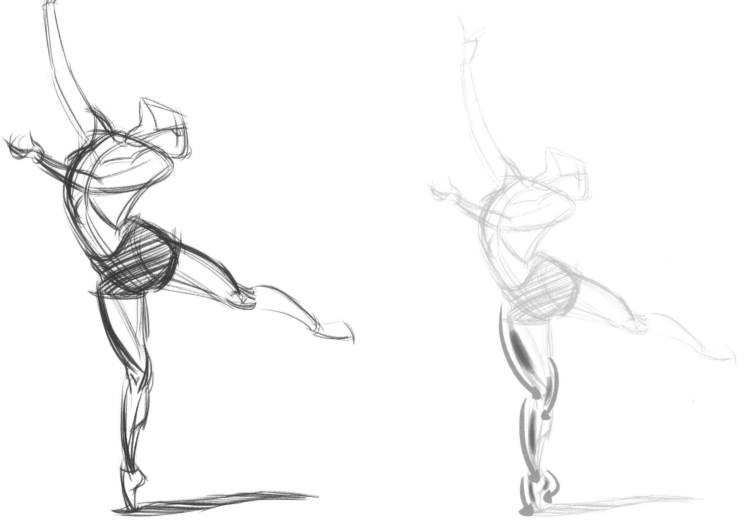

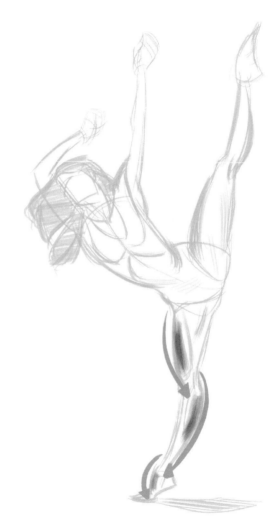

*Notice the effort in this athlete's right leg to support her weight, indicated by the areas of **Applied FORCE**.*

*I use the strong **Applied FORCEs** in this athlete's arms to emphasize the energy and effort that he uses to climb the rope.*

I like the amount of power in this dancer's left arm as it presses against the floor and supports the weight of her upper torso, head and right arm. Notice the areas of **Applied** and *Directional FORCE*.

This figure's arms are under an insane amount of tension to hold his whole body in position. Look at all the Applied FORCEs.

*What excites me to draw this action is showing all the energy and effort that goes into it. Notice the **Applied FORCEs** in her arms, abdomen and glutes as she holds her body in position.*

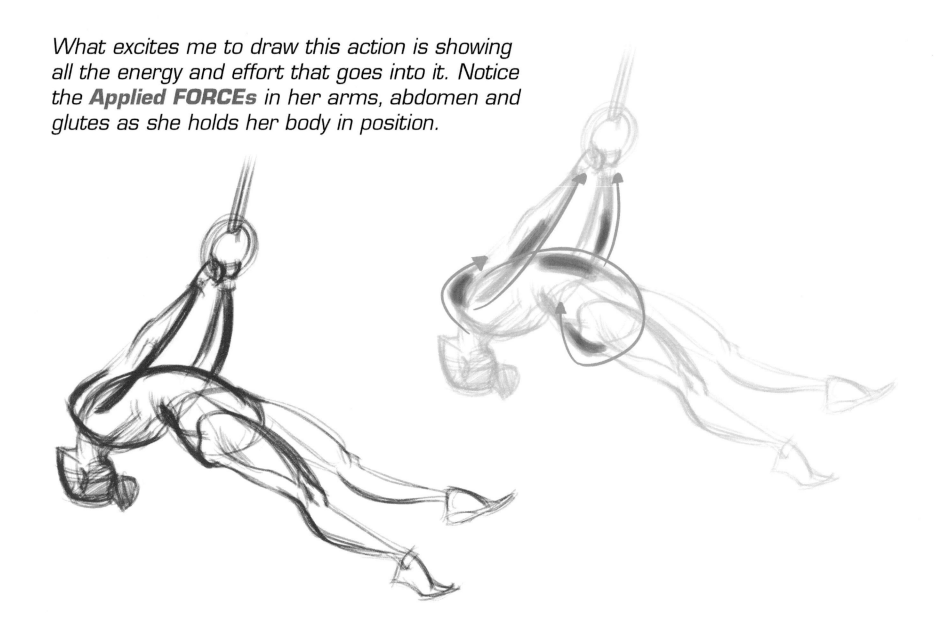

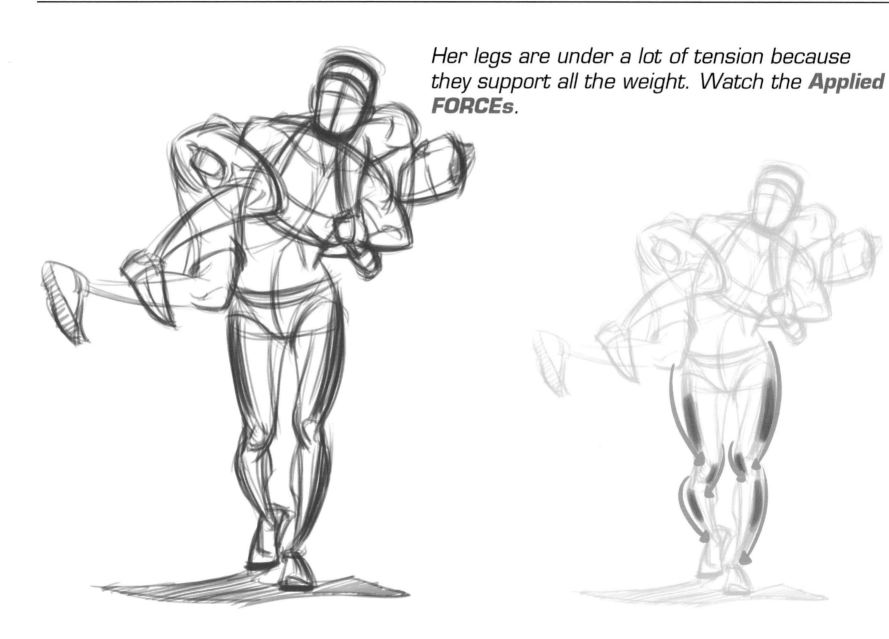

Her legs are under a lot of tension because they support all the weight. Watch the **Applied FORCEs**.

*Imagine yourself in this pose, and feel all the effort it takes to maintain it for a couple of seconds. The areas of **Applied FORCE** indicate where you would feel the most tension in your muscles.*

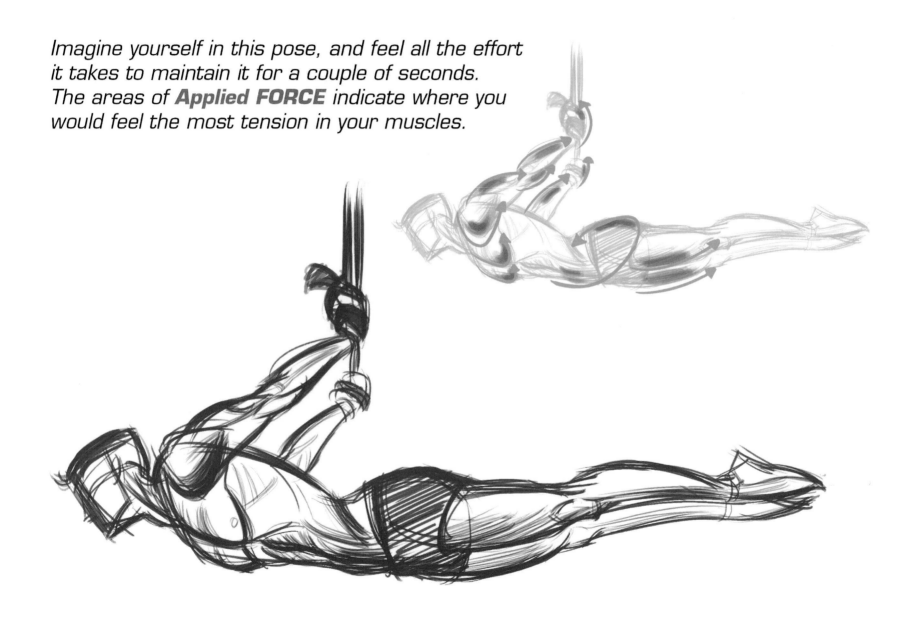

I use **Applied FORCE** to capture the effort that this athlete puts into his whole body to lift the heavy weights. I also exaggerate the bend of the bar and add darker lines at the bottom of the weights to emphasize the pull of **Gravity**.

THE LEADING EDGE

The Leading Edge is the edge of the body that leads an action. Here you will find the greatest amount of Applied FORCE. A great place to start your drawing is with the Leading Edge.

 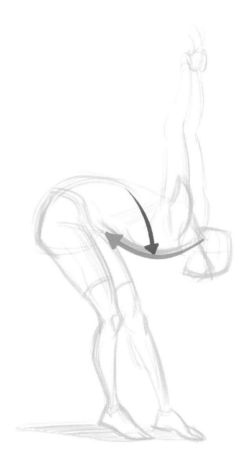

*My starting point for this drawing is the **Directional FORCE** thrusting from her back into her left shoulder. This is the **Leading Edge** of the action.*

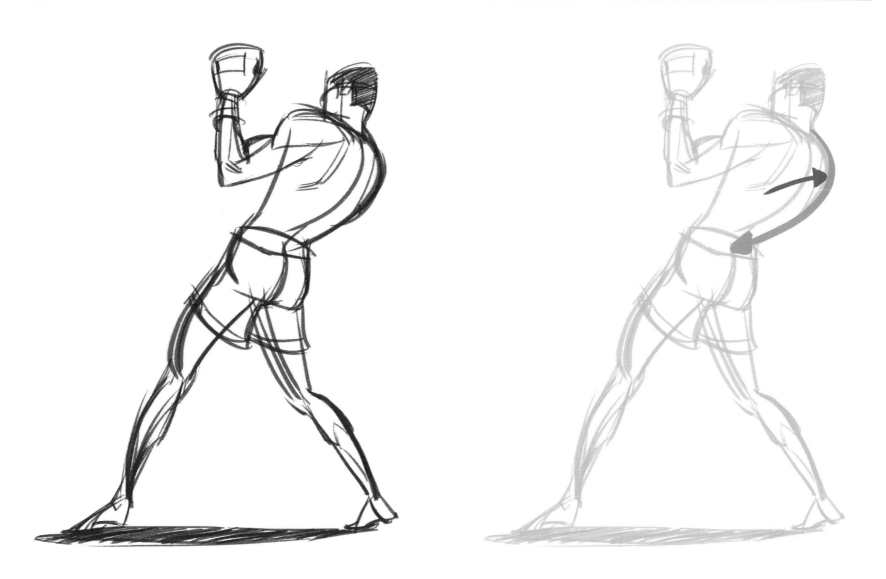

Here, the **Leading Edge** is the boxer's back as he leans to the right. This is the first **Directional FORCE** I draw.

*The **Leading Edge** clarifies the direction of the figure's movement.*

*In the action below, the **Leading Edge** is found in the gymnast's right hip.*

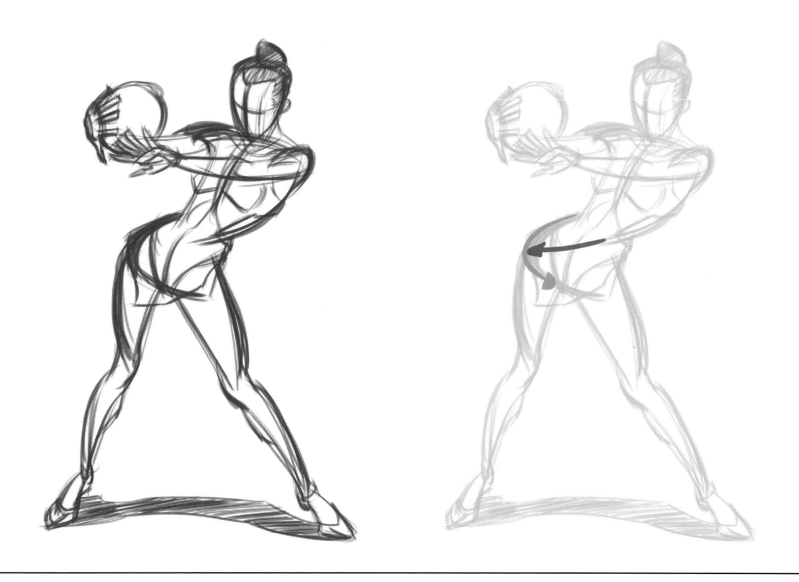

To draw this dancer I go for the clear Leading Edge of her rib cage. I use darker lines in that area to indicate the great amount of Applied FORCE that pushes her forward.

*The **Leading Edge** in this athlete's left shoulder gives her a clear direction of movement. I use darker lines in that area to clarify this.*

Watch how the Leading Edge shifts from the martial artist's left shoulder to his right elbow in this motion study.

When you do motion studies, pay special attention to the *Leading Edge* in each frame of action.

THE ROAD OF RHYTHM

A Directional FORCE either becomes an Applied FORCE (1), Continues (2) or Splits (3). Directional FORCE never hops on one side of the body!

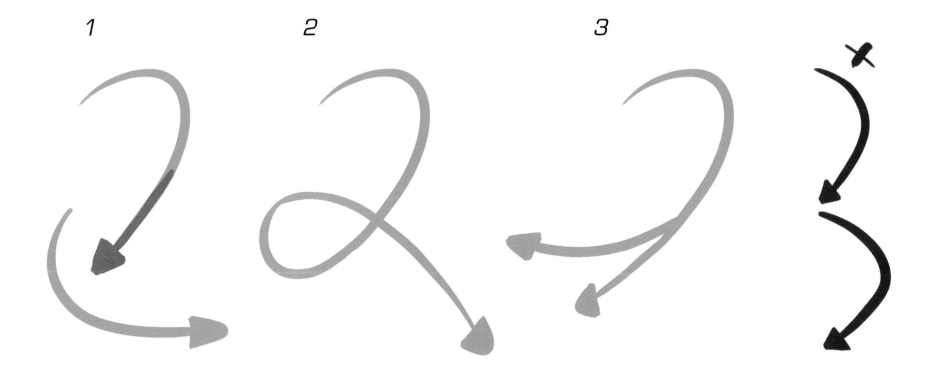

1   2   3

Remember that a single *Directional FORCE* is a *C-curve*, not an **S-curve**.

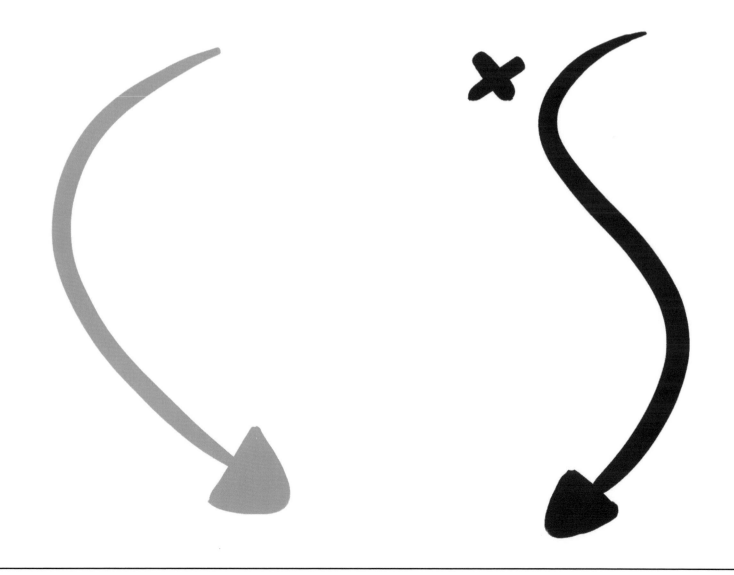

*To get an S-curve, you need two related **Directional FORCEs**. This is called a **Rhythm**.*

*To recap, one line or idea is a Directional FORCE (1). **Two** Directional FORCEs create **one** Rhythm (2).*

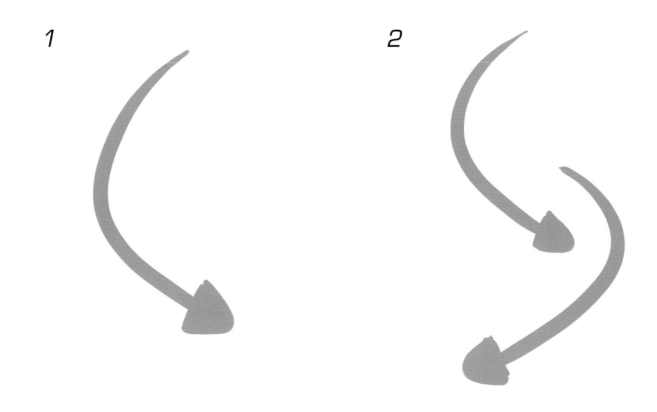

*Below, diagram 1 has one **Rhythm**, diagram 2 has two **Rhythms** and diagram 3 has four **Rhythms**.*

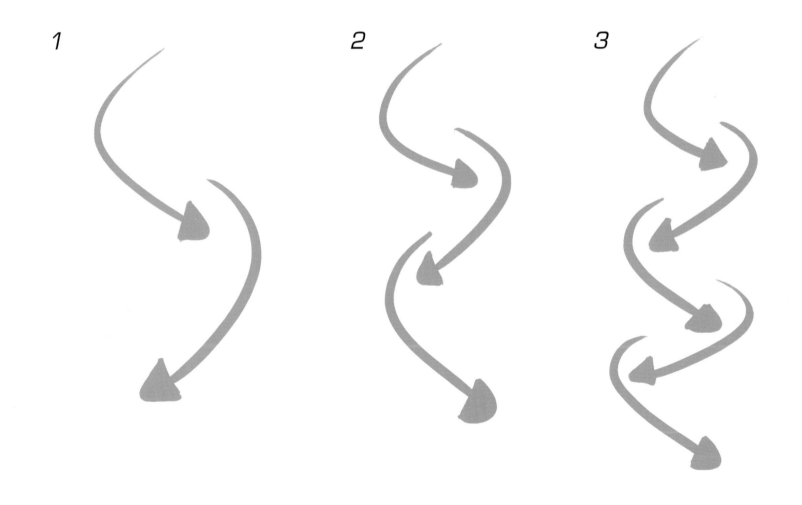

1   2   3

Rhythm helps the masses of the body stay balanced against **Gravity**. **Hopping** on one side of the body doesn't create balance.

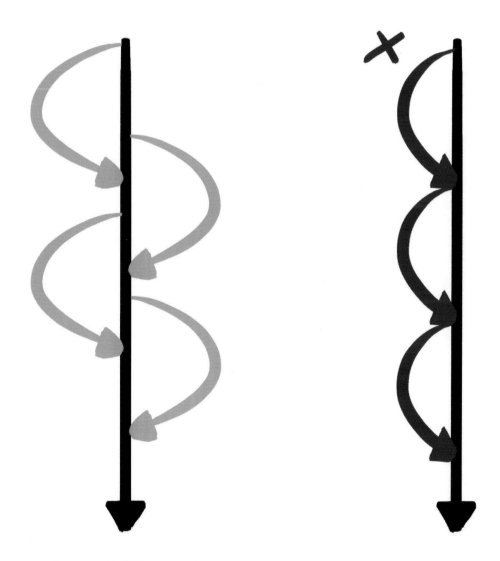

This left-to-right interplay of energies in the body is also referred to as the **Road of Rhythm**. *It's a more flat, two-dimensional approach to understand the body's fluid-like balance.*

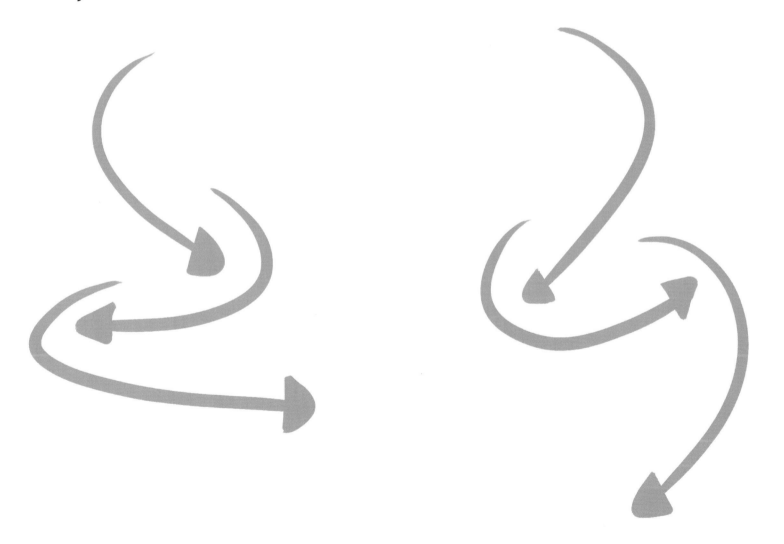

Observe and draw the Directional FORCEs *as they occur in reality. What is the degree of curvature? Where is the peak of each curve? Avoid* **generic curves**.

The figure's torso works as an **S-curve** (1) or a **C-curve** (2), depending on the action. Observe the *Directional FORCEs* for both functions.

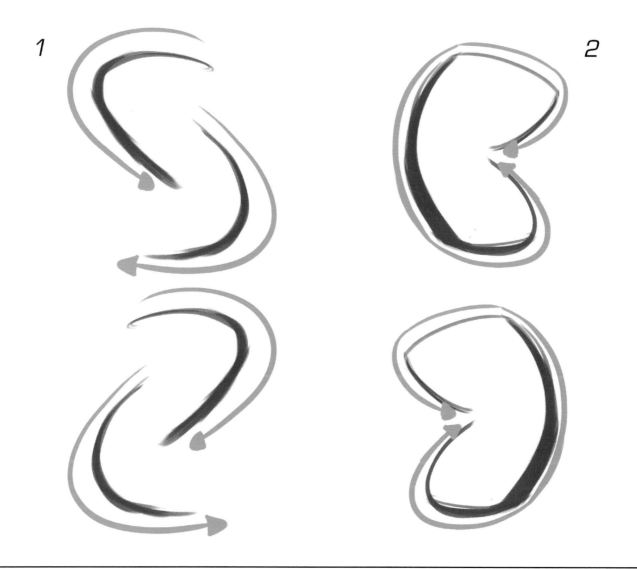

*The **Directional FORCEs** of the torso form a clear **S-curve** in this pose.*

*In this drawing, my focus is the clear **S-curve** created by the **Directional FORCEs** of this model's rib cage and pelvis.*

*When the torso bends, its **Directional FORCE** is a clear **C-curve**.*

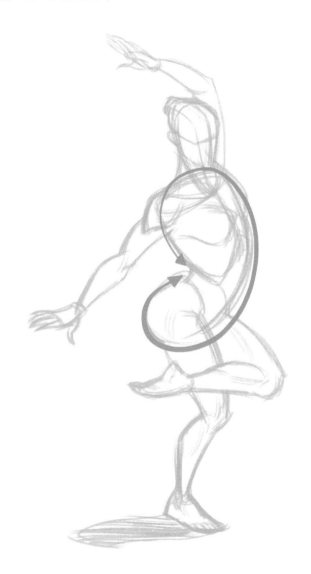

Here's another example of how the **Directional FORCE** of the model's bending torso forms a clear **C-curve**.

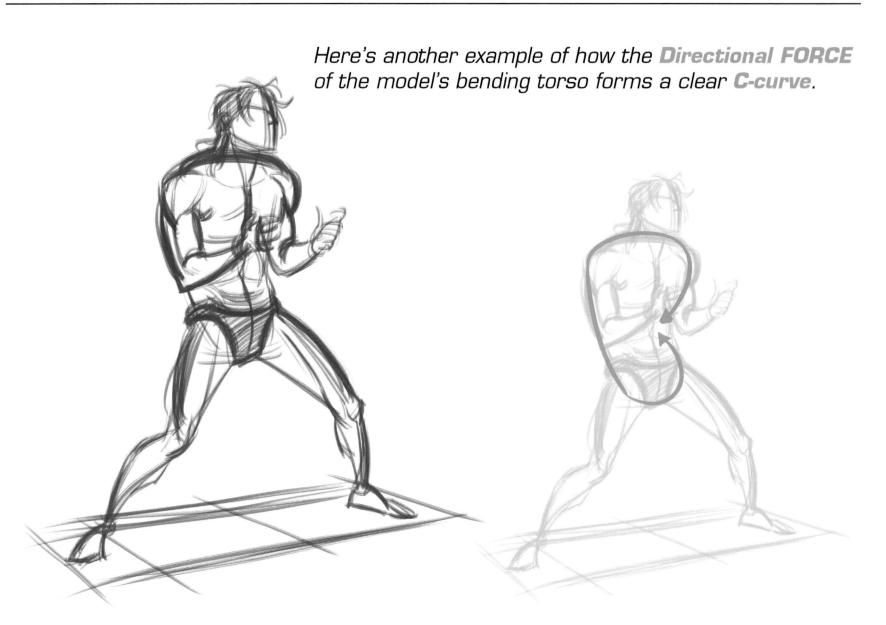

*Regardless of the action of the torso, drive **Directional FORCE** around its top and bottom to get a sense of its mass. This gives you a good basis to attach the limbs.*

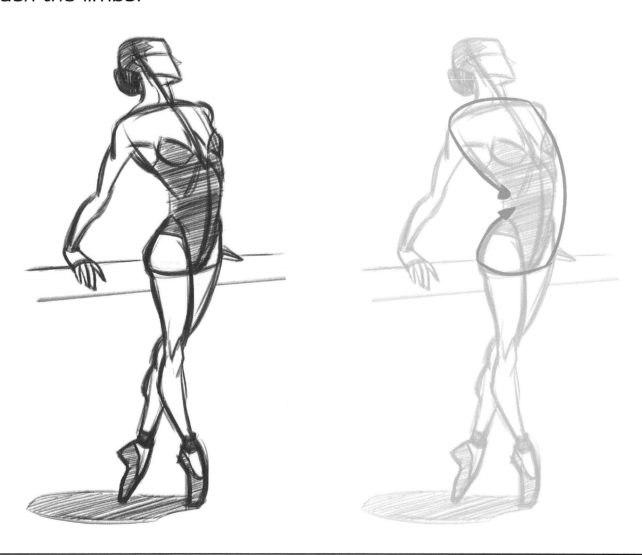

*Here we take our first step out of the **Directional FORCE** of the torso and connect it to the rest of the body through **Rhythm**.*

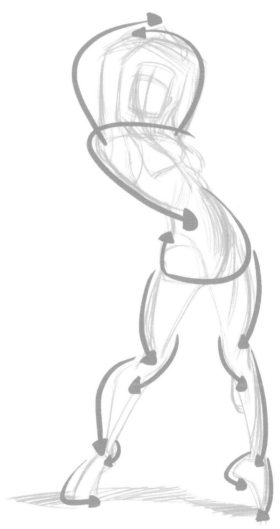

*To me, short time limits are not to check how fast I can draw but to practice **Hierarchy**. Hierarchy refers to order of importance. What is the action about? And what should I draw first to communicate that?*

*One-minute drawings are great to loosen up. Use **Rhythm** to drive through the whole body and capture the action.*

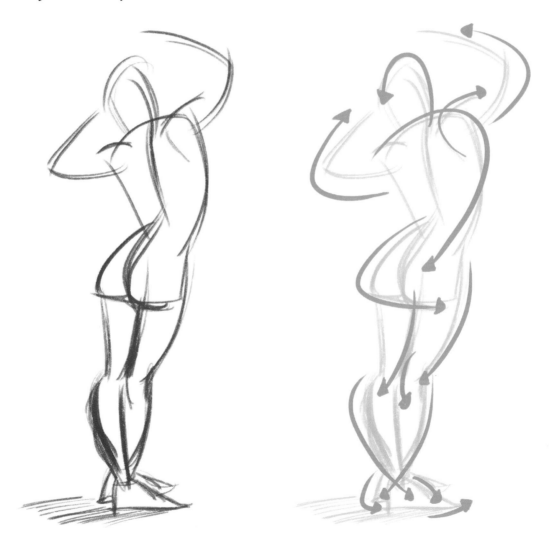

*Here's a one-minute drawing. I find the **Directional FORCEs** and how they create a **Road of Rhythm** through the body.*

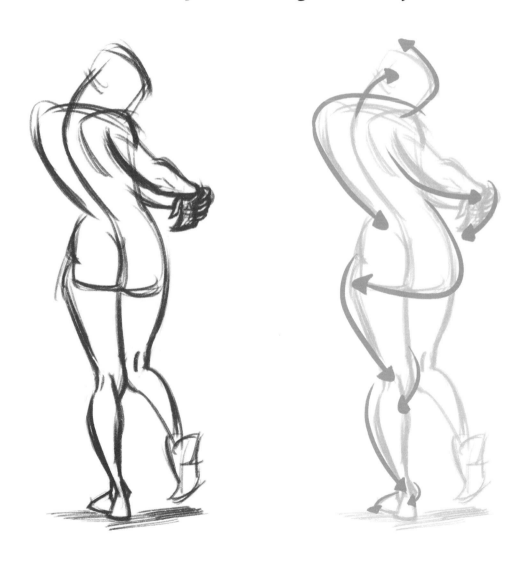

*Two or more related Directional FORCEs create Rhythm. Rhythm enables the human body to stay balanced relative to **Gravity**.*

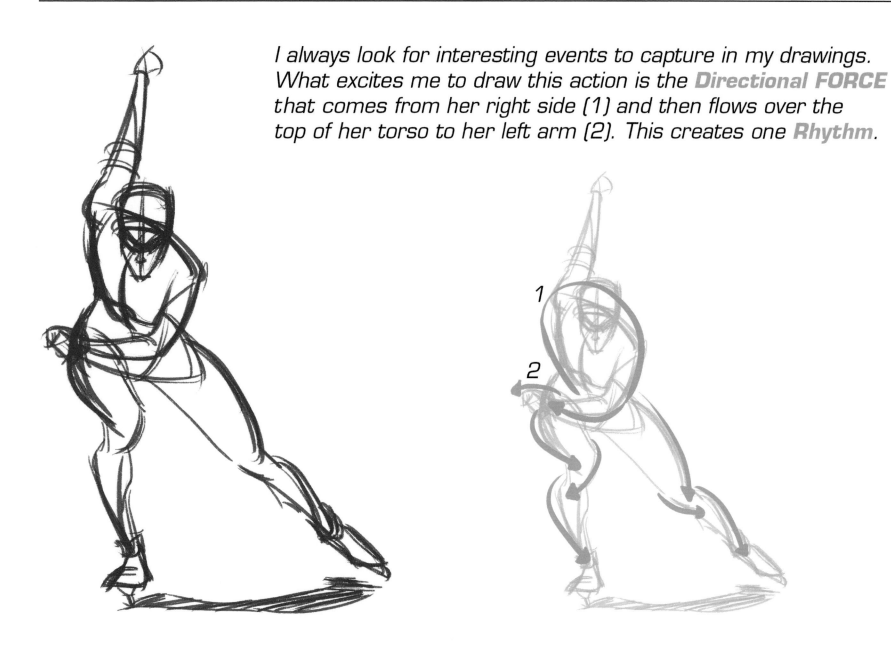

I always look for interesting events to capture in my drawings. What excites me to draw this action is the Directional FORCE that comes from her right side (1) and then flows over the top of her torso to her left arm (2). This creates one Rhythm.

Look at the **Rhythm** created by the **Directional FORCE** that drives through her back over her right shoulder (1) and shoots toward us through her upper arm (2) before it recedes in space to her hand (3).

*I like the strong bend (1) in this athlete's torso in contrast to the **straightness** of his legs. Notice that his legs still have Rhythm!*

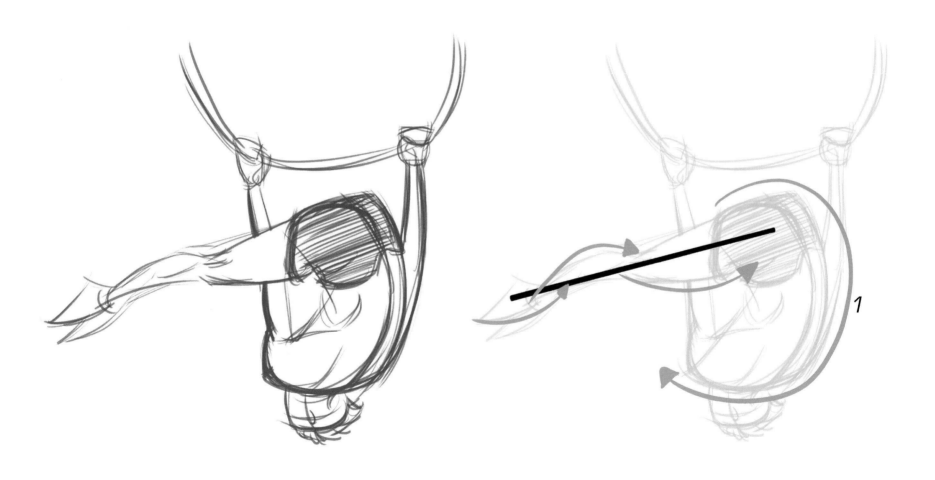

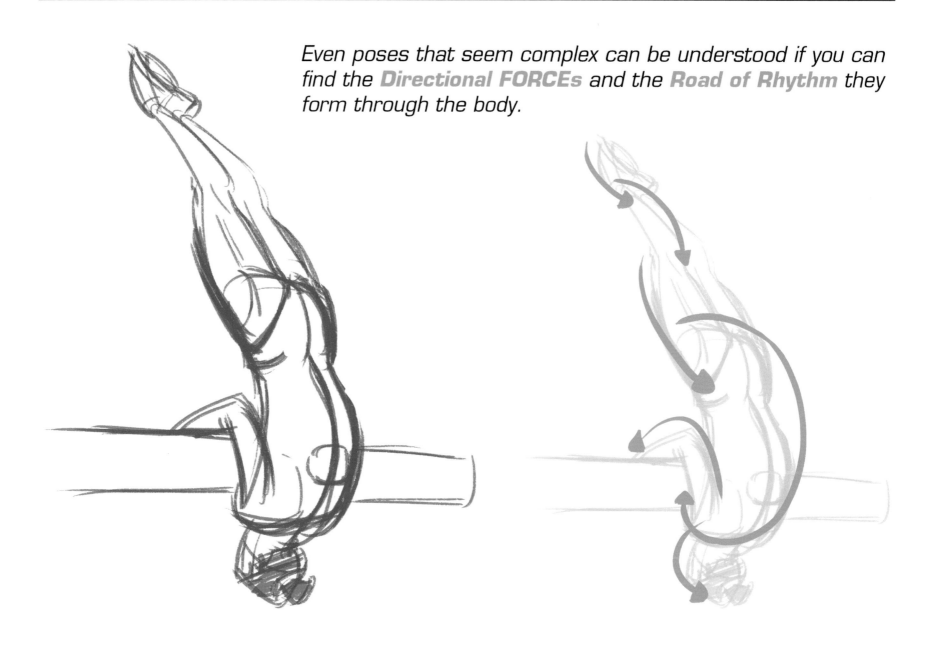

Even poses that seem complex can be understood if you can find the **Directional FORCEs** and the **Road of Rhythm** they form through the body.

*Notice how **Directional FORCE** flows from this skater's spine into her neck and head. If you miss this **Rhythm**, the head and neck will most likely end up looking disconnected from the body.*

*Here again, look at the **Rhythm** between this model's spine and her face.*

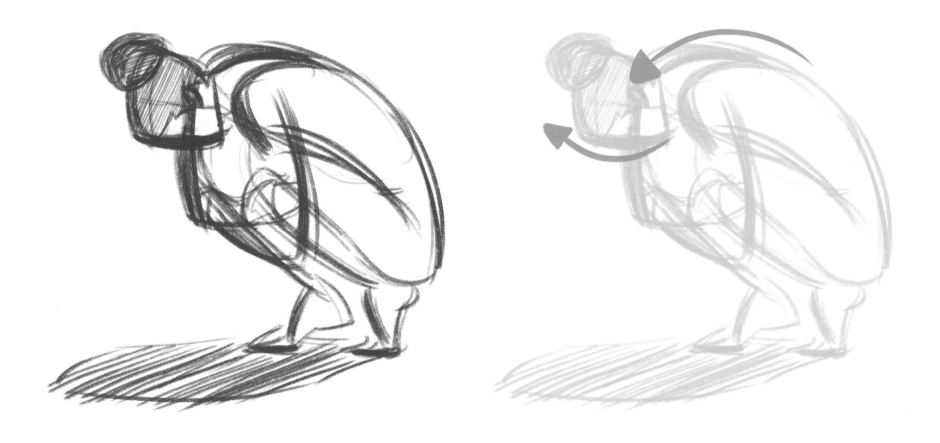

*Look for the **Directional FORCE** of the neck created by the sternocleidomastoid muscle (1). It forms a **Rhythm** with the upper torso and helps you connect the head.*

*The **Directional FORCE** of the upper arm is created by the triceps, **not the biceps**. This is very evident in a body builder's arm. Observe how big the curve of the triceps is compared with the biceps. Whether the arm is muscular or lean, this **Directional FORCE** remains the same.*

*Below is the drawing of an arm rotated toward the body. Notice that the arm works as **one** (1) simple Directional FORCE curve. Watch out for **dysfunctional Rhythms**.*

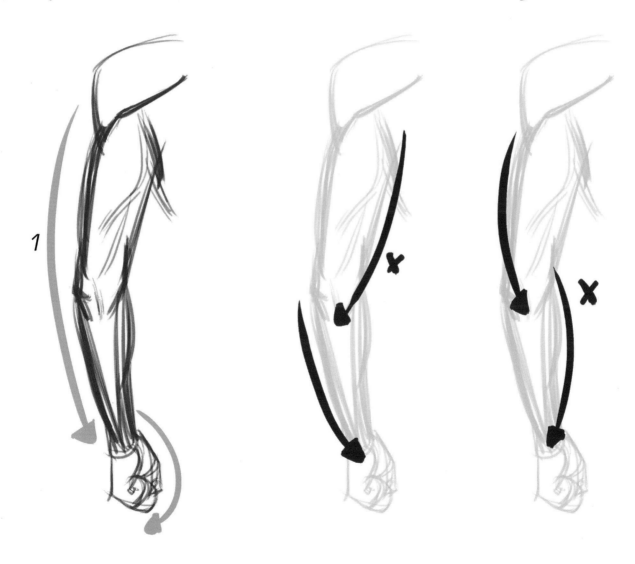

*Below is the drawing of an arm rotated away from the body. Again, notice the **one** (1) simple Directional FORCE, and watch out for **dysfunctional Rhythms**.*

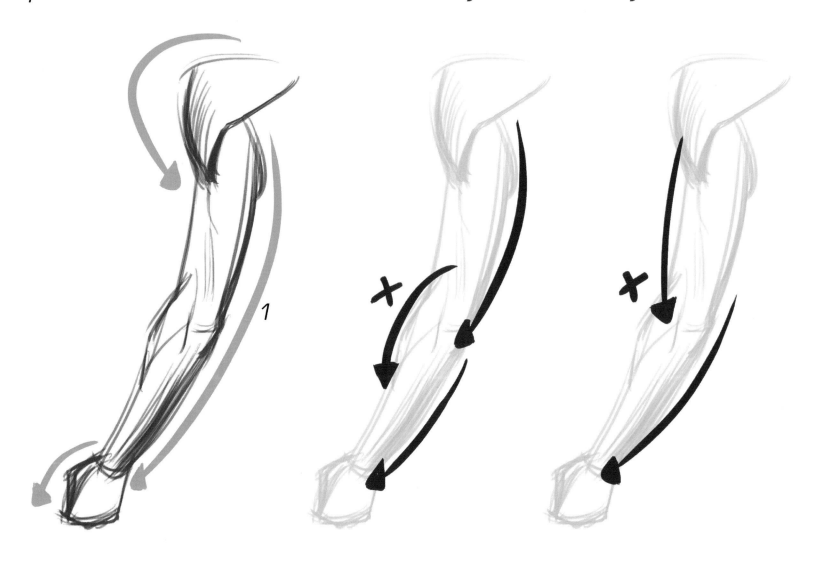

*When the arm is **hyperextended** at the elbow joint it goes from one (1) to **three** (1, 2, 3) Directional FORCEs.*

Observe the simple **Rhythms** of the arms in this motion study. Remember the rules on the previous pages.

I like the sense of power in this athlete's arms as she holds up the tire. I use **Applied FORCE** *to capture this. Notice the different arm functions, which is made clear by their* **Rhythms**.

*Observe how **Directional FORCE** drives from the forearm (1), around the palm of the hand (2) toward the fingers (3). This creates two **Rhythms**.*

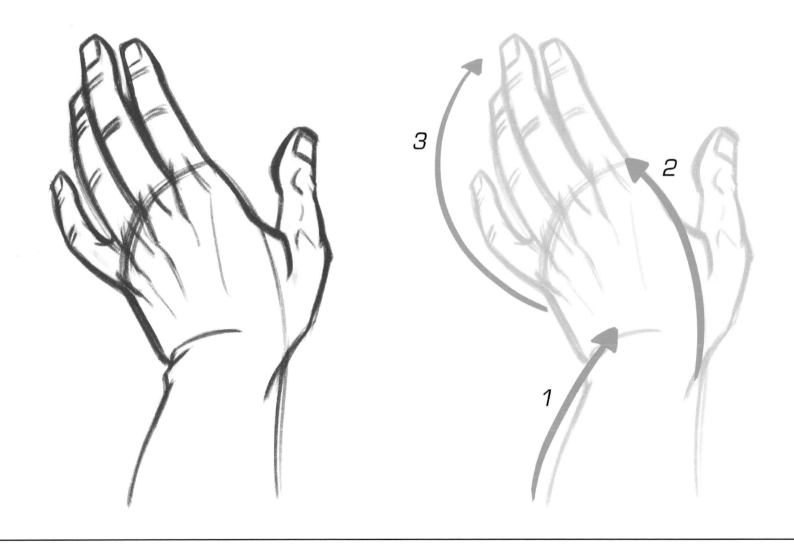

Here, the forearm and hand work as one *Directional FORCE* (1). Notice the *Rhythms* of the fingers.

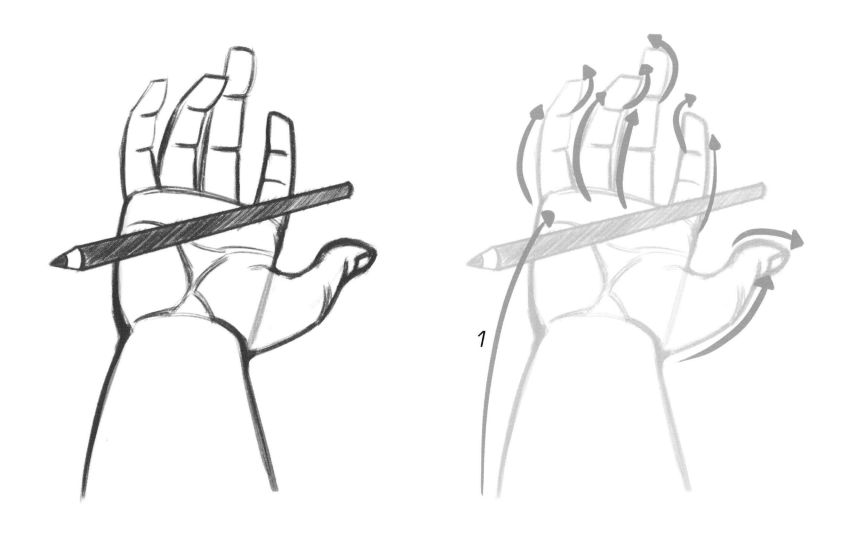

1

*Notice the **FORCE Curve** (1) at the front of her left leg as it supports all her weight and builds up energy (like a compressed spring) to launch her body forward.*
This sense of anticipation gets me excited to draw this action.

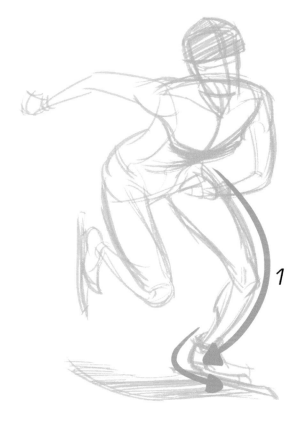

*Keep in mind that there is one **Directional FORCE** between two joints.*

This rugby player's left leg **launches him into the air**, while his right leg bends like a metal bar and prepares to catch his weight once he lands. Notice the *Rhythms*.

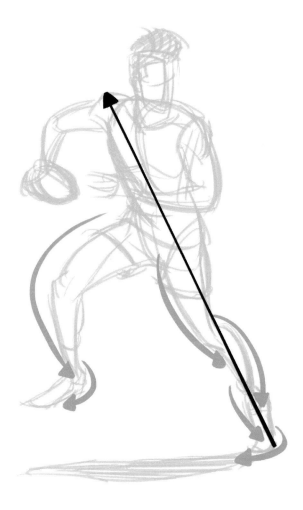

*This athlete's bending leg works as one **FORCE Curve** (1) in contrast to the **Rhythms** of his kicking leg.*

*Watch the different **Rhythms** of the rugby player's legs based on their function during the action.*

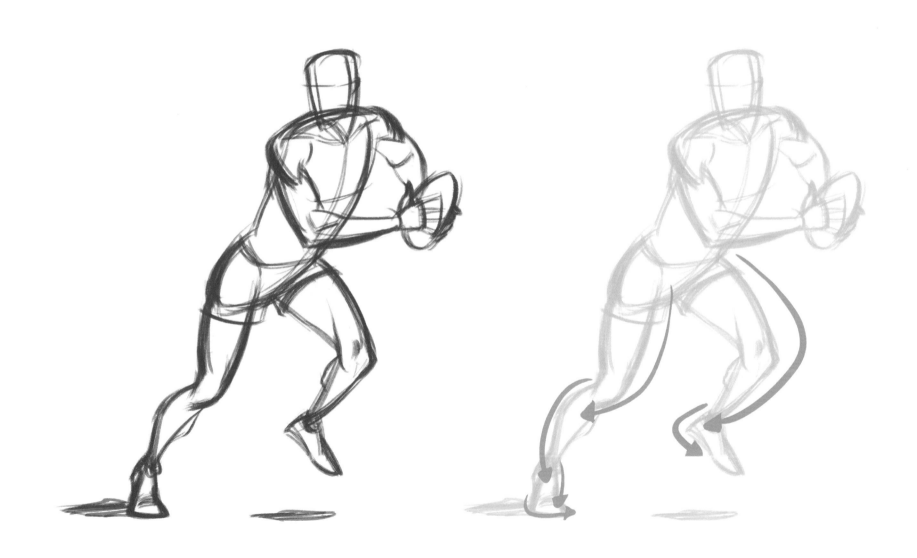

*Here, I use **Rhythm** to capture the sense of speed in the model's right leg.*

*Observe the **Rhythms** and **Applied FORCEs** of this gymnast's weight-supporting leg.*

I emphasize this gymnast's massive, muscular legs and put some extra work into her left leg to show that it supports all her weight. Notice the **Rhythms** *and* ***Applied FORCEs.***

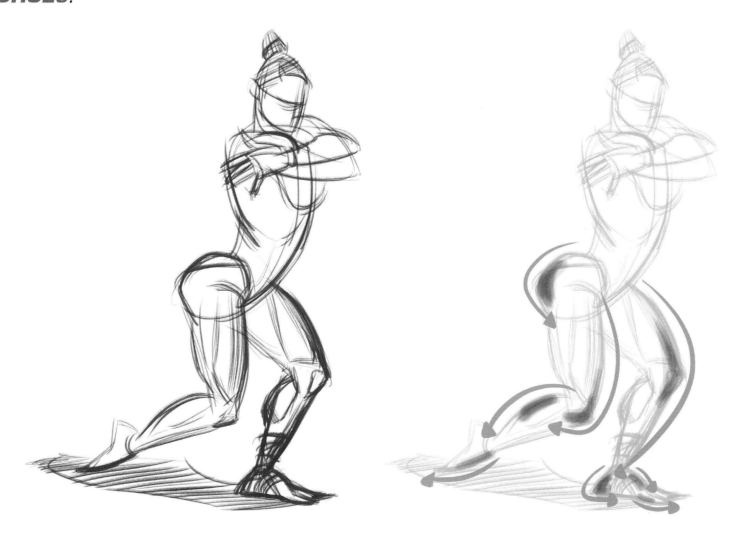

*The foot's **Rhythms** help you understand how it works.*

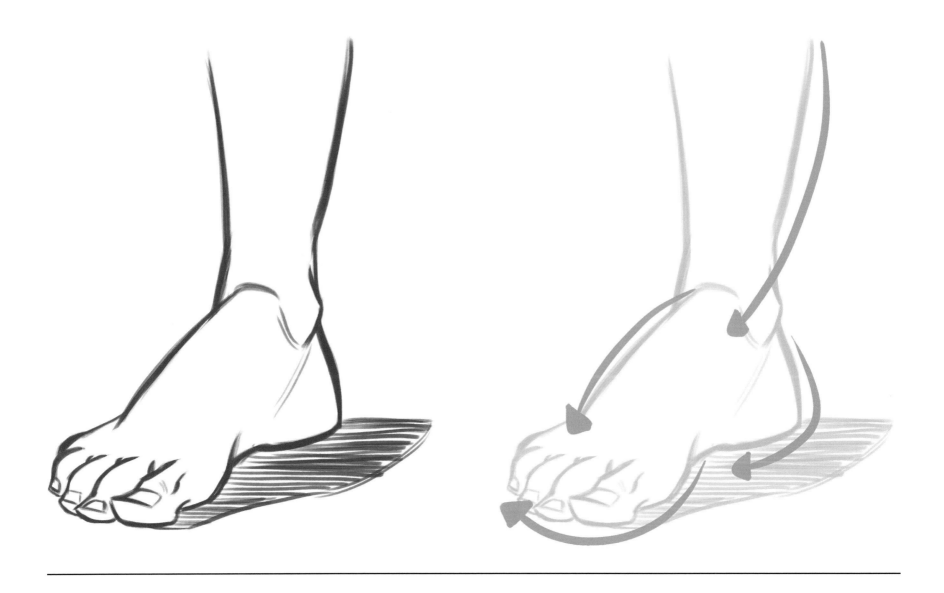

The **Directional FORCEs** create a sense of **Rhythm** and fluidity in the foot. They also make all the parts feel connected.

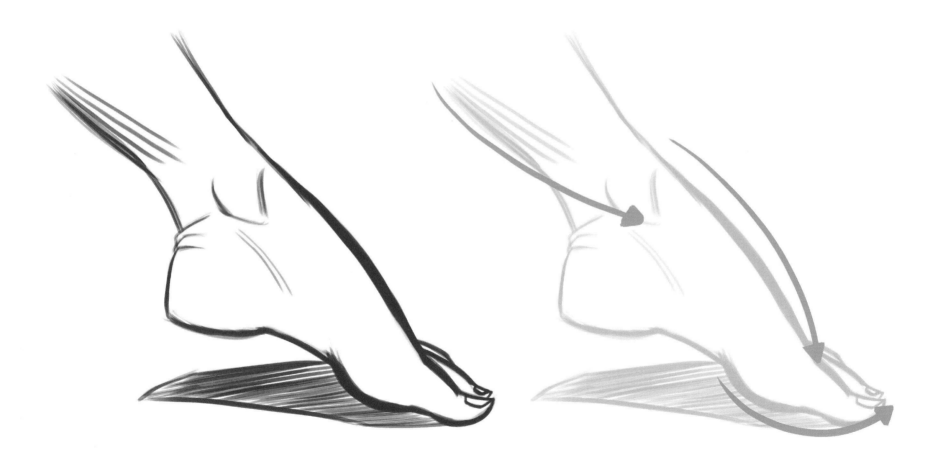

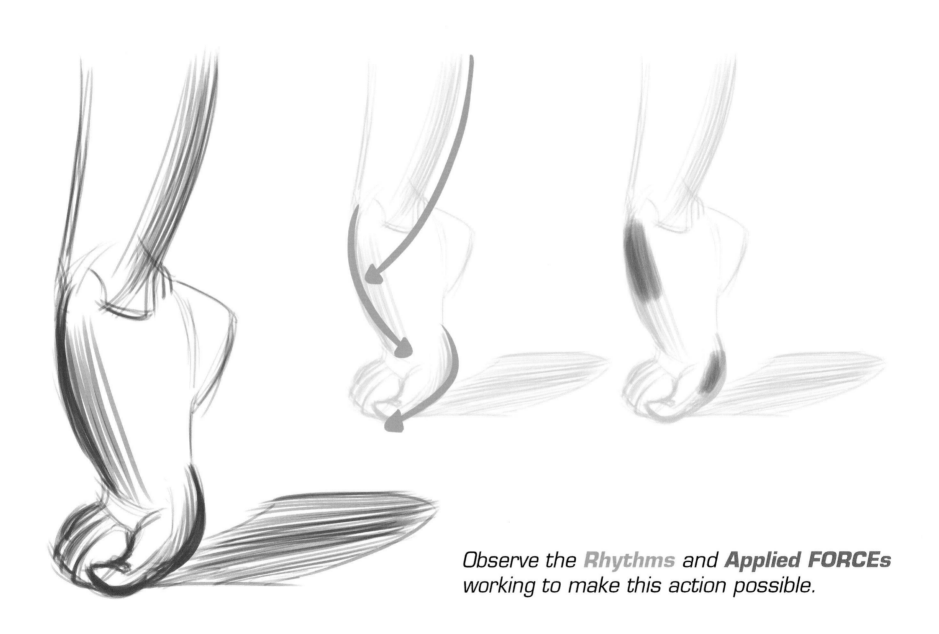

*Observe the **Rhythms** and **Applied FORCEs** working to make this action possible.*

Directional FORCE creates Rhythm as it travels over the top of the foot (1), **applies** *itself to the ball of the foot (2), and finally shoots out of the big toe (3).* *Be aware of* **Gravity***.*

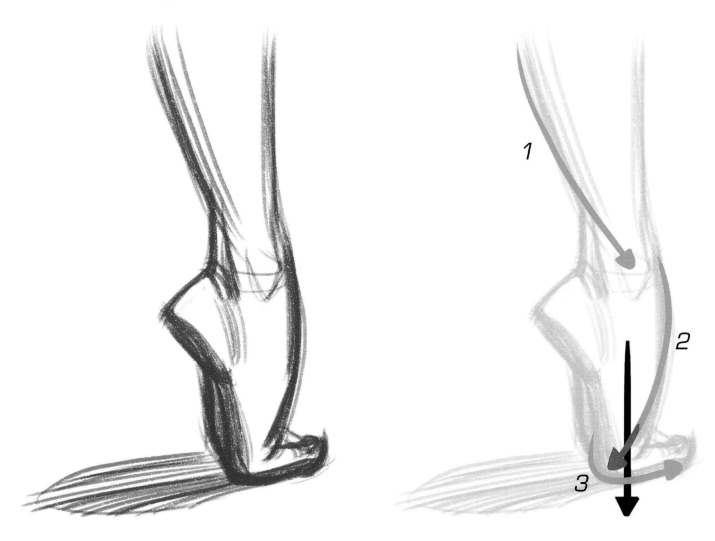

THE ROLLER COASTER OF RHYTHM

*The **Roller Coaster of Rhythm** deals with how FORCE moves in a three-dimensional manner through and around the figure. Compare this to a roller coaster ride in an amusement park.*

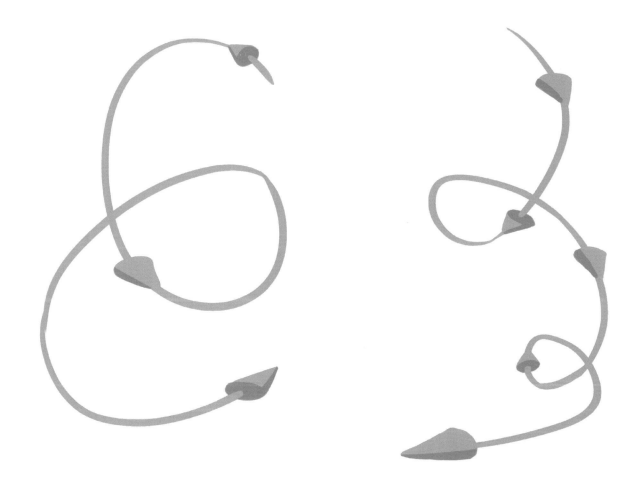

If I **merge** the Directional FORCE of the model's torso with that of his left leg, I lose the anatomical function. Notice that I follow the Rhythms from his back to his belly, around the bottom of his pelvis, over his hip bones and then into his leg.

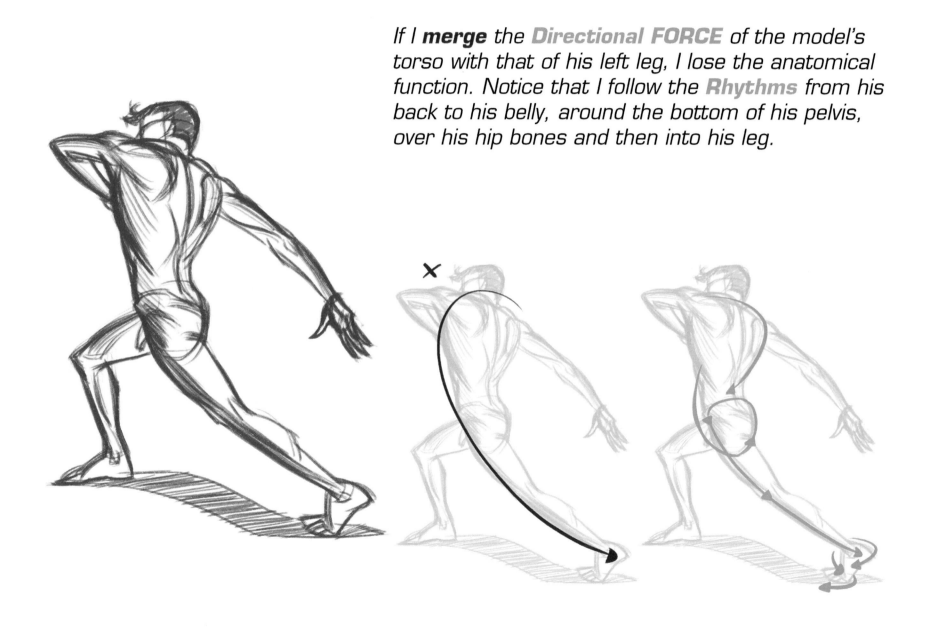

Notice how **Directional FORCE** travels from this model's left hand (1), up around her torso (2) and finally shoots down out of her right thigh (3). It creates a clear **Roller Coaster of Rhythm** that connects all these body parts.

*FORCE is about function. The primary function we look for in the figure is balance relative to **Gravity**. The position of the model's right leg is very important to support the weight of his bending torso. If he removes that leg from underneath his torso, he will lose his balance and fall.*

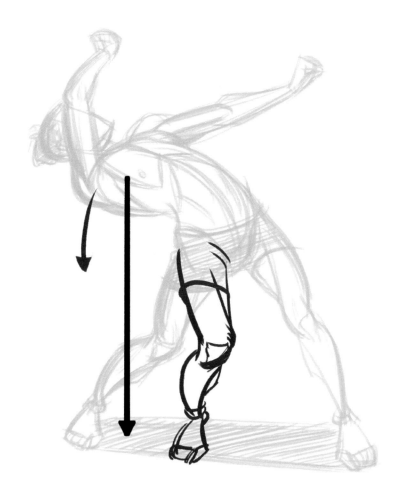

*I like all the **Applied FORCE** that goes into bending this gymnast's torso so she can lift her right leg. The **Directional FORCEs** create **Rhythm**, which helps her stay balanced relative to **Gravity**.*

*I use darker lines on this gymnast's shoulders and arms to show how hard they work to hold his weight against the pull of **Gravity**. Notice the Directional FORCEs and **Applied FORCEs** at work.*

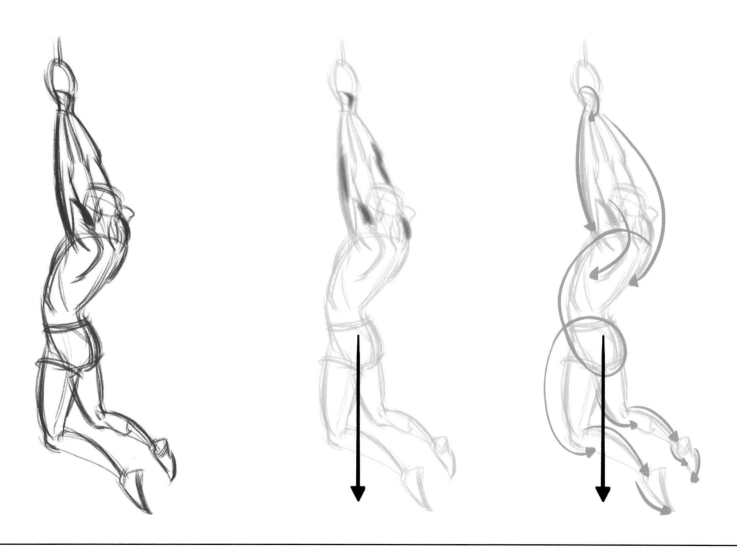

Here, I show the **Applied FORCE** that leads her body to her left and the **Applied FORCEs** in her left leg, which supports her weight. Notice how the **Directional FORCEs** create **Rhythm** and help her stay balanced against **Gravity**.

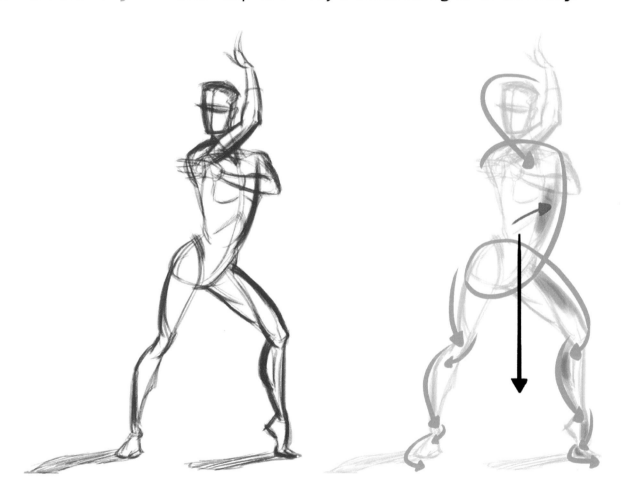

The strong **Applied FORCE** in her upper torso gives this action a clear direction of movement.
Notice the *Directional FORCEs*, which help her stay balanced against **Gravity** through *Rhythm*.

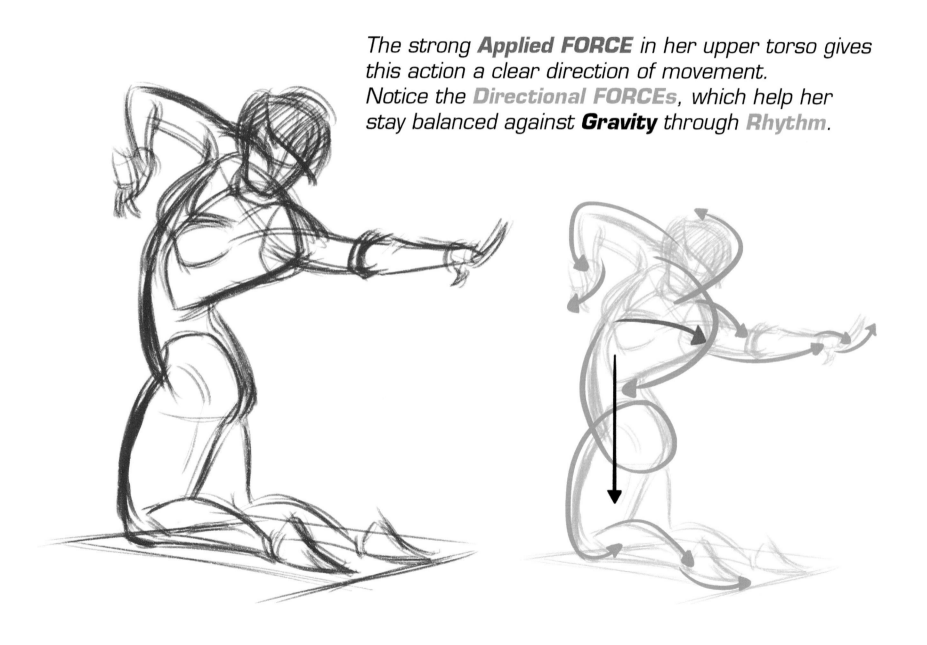

Chapter 2
FORCE Form

PERSPECTIVE

*The first step to drawing Form is to learn the basics of **Perspective**.*
*Below are boxes in a **One**-, **Two**-, **Three**- and **Four-Point** Perspectives.*

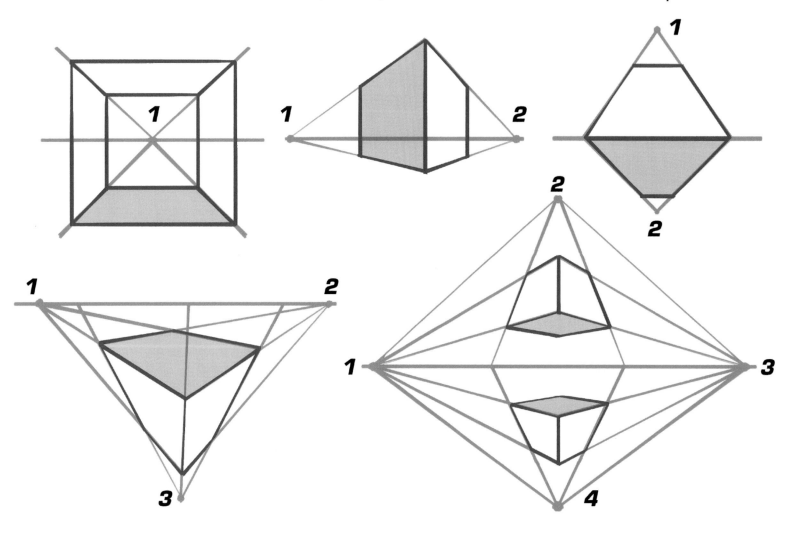

If we look at the front side of a box, we cannot see another of its sides at the same time. This is a **Fake/Orthographic Perspective** (A). In order to see another side of this box, we need **Two Points** as reference (B).

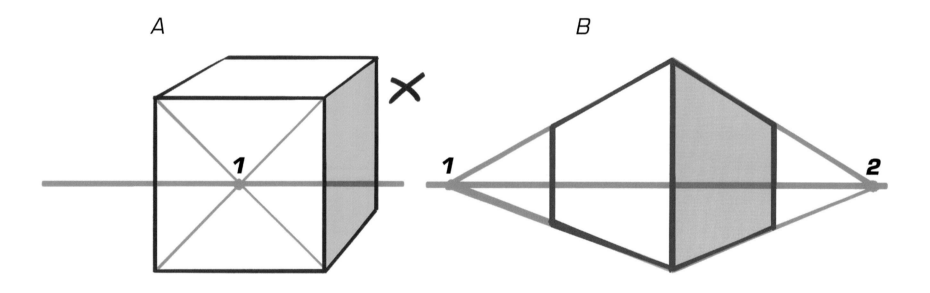

Learn to draw a box in any Perspective from your imagination. This is essential if you want to draw well.

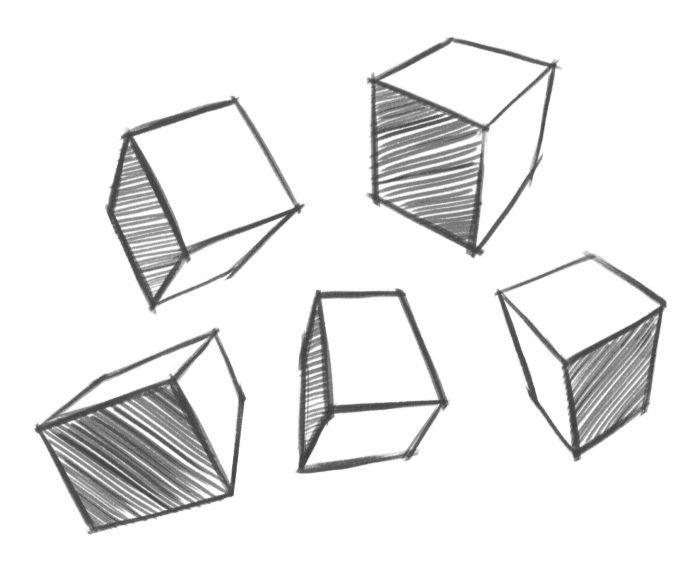

*We look down at the model in this pose. This is called a bird's-eye view. I relate her to a **box** to help me get the Three-Point Perspective right.*

*I visualize a **box** around the foreshortened pose of this athlete to help me understand the Two-Point Perspective.*

*This is another case in which we look down at the figure in a Three-Point Perspective. I visualize her standing in a **box** to help me place her in space.*

*Relate the head to a **box** to help you draw its Structure properly.*

Here's another example of how I relate the head to a **box** to help me get the Structure and Perspective right.

*I pay attention to the **Perspective Angles** to help me draw this athlete.*

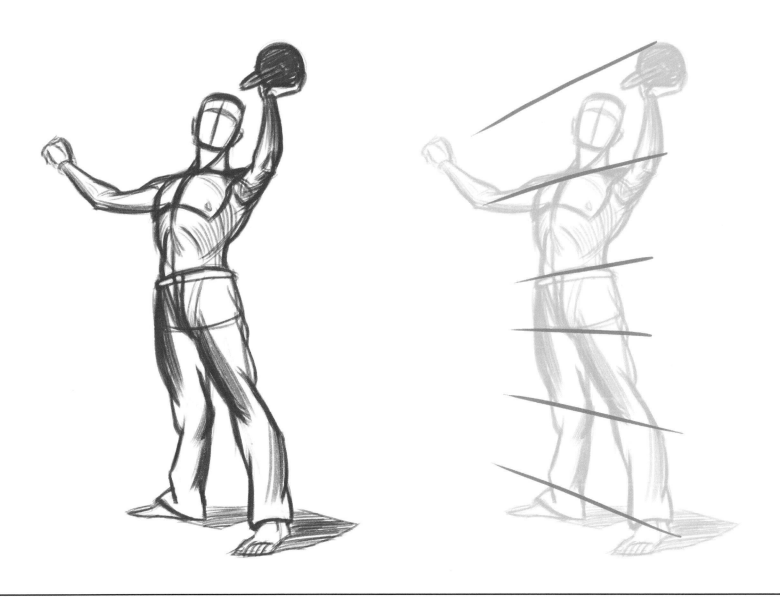

In this case, we look up at this gymnast. This is called a worm's-eye view.
I visualize the **Perspective Angles** to help me draw her correctly.

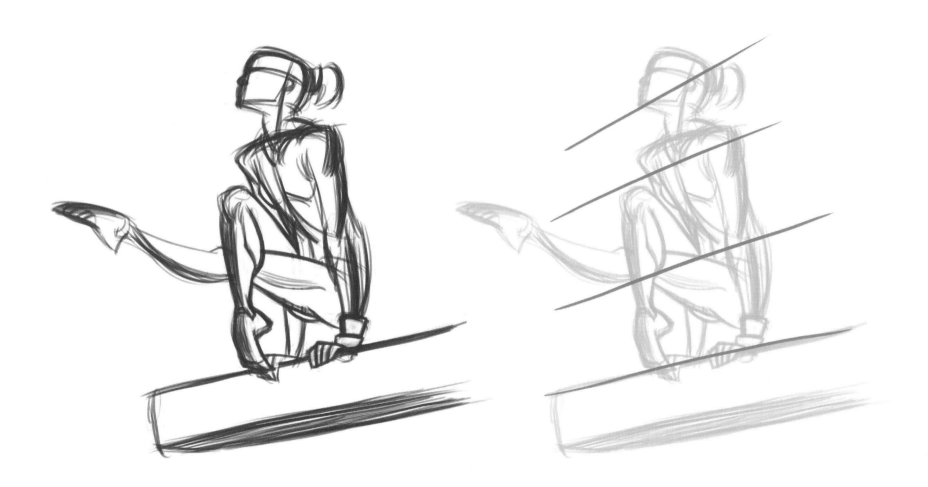

*Here, the Horizon is at her ankles (1). The **Perspective Angles** become more diagonal as they approach her head (2).*

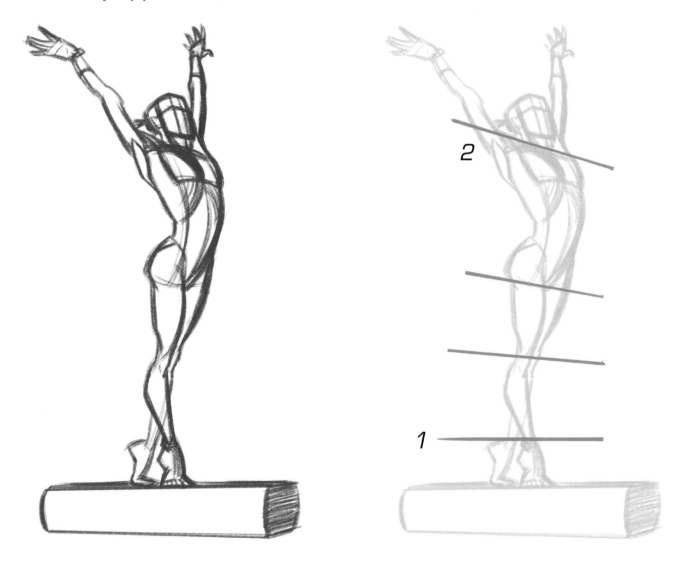

The Two-Point **Perspective Grid** helps me place the model's legs and right hand.

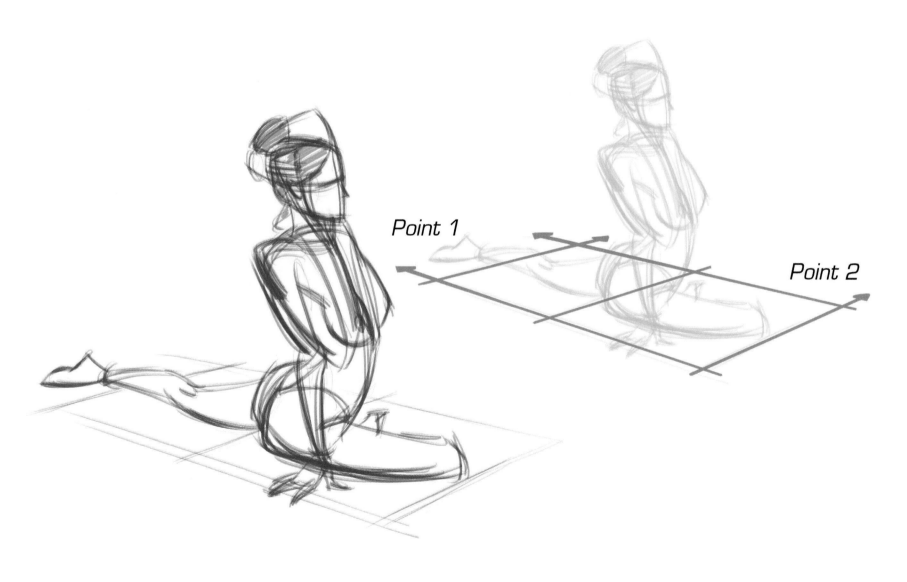

Point 1

Point 2

*I draw a Two-Point Perspective Grid to establish a **Ground Plane** and help me get a sense of space. This is useful when you deal with foreshortened poses.*

Drawing the **Ground Plane** comes in handy when the figure lies on the floor.

The **Ground Plane** helps me understand the placement of the model's arm and legs in three-dimensional space.

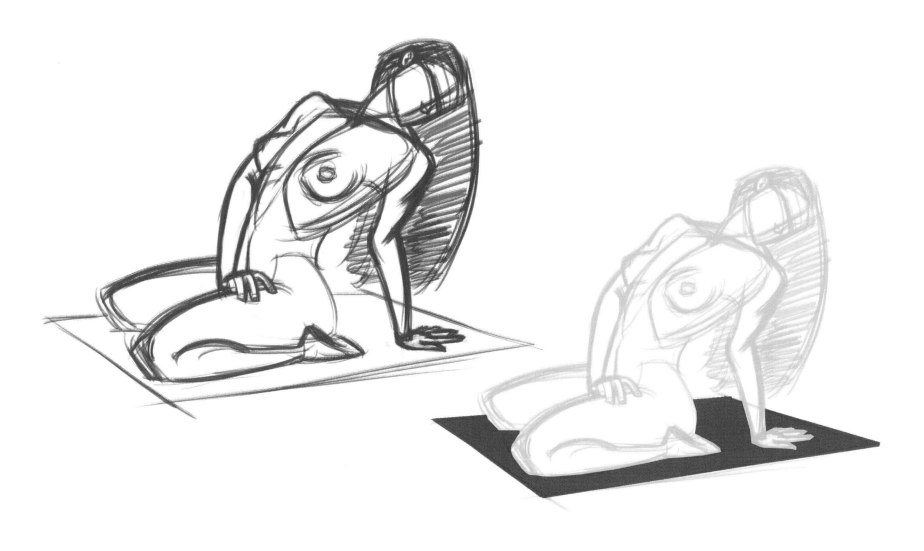

*Here, the **Ground Plane** helps me understand the placement of the model's feet.*

Now we transition from the Ground Plane (A) to the **Base**. The **Base** is defined by the body's touchpoints to the Ground Plane.

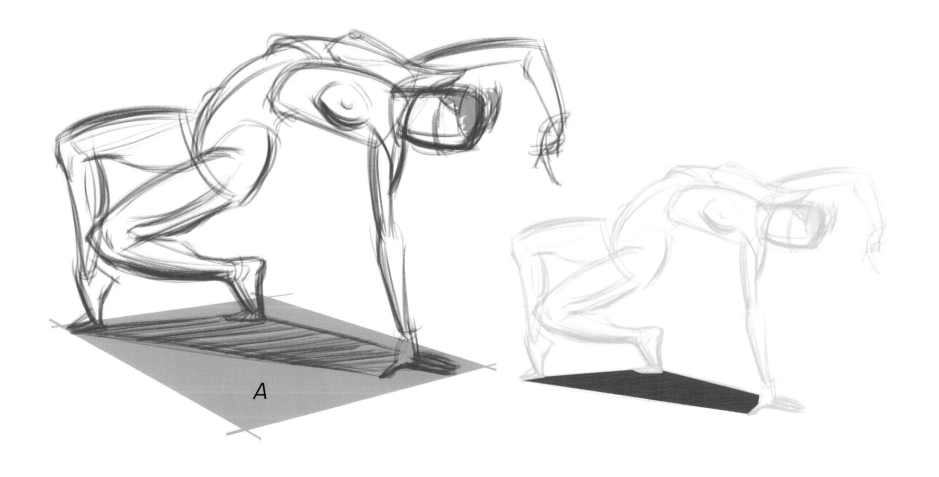

A

Here, I use the gymnast's **Base** to help me get the Perspective right.

*I connect the model's hands and feet with straight lines to find their placement in three-dimensional space. This creates the model's **base**.*

THE TURNING EDGE

*The **Turning Edge** is the edge between two planes (1 and 2) of a Form. The simplest example is a box Form. Notice the **Turning Edges** of the boxes below.*

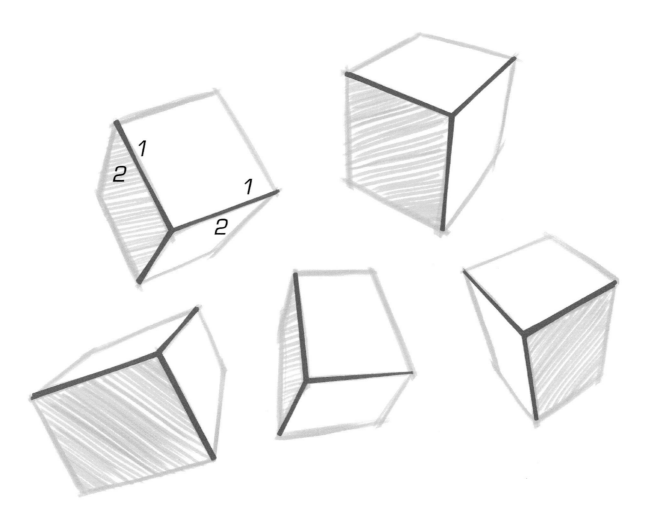

*Here, the **Turning Edge** helps me draw this gymnast's twisting torso.*

*The **Turning Edge** of the model's torso helps me understand its orientation in space.*

*I look for the **Turning Edge** of this athlete's torso to help me get a sense of its volume and slight twist.*

This pose has a great sense of balance. I draw the **Turning Edge** of the martial artist's torso to help me get a sense of its Structure.

*The **Turning Edges** of the athlete's back and head help me define their planes (1, 2 and 3).*

*I draw the **Turning Edges** of this gymnast's head, torso and legs to help me understand their orientation in space.*

*The **Turning Edge** helps me define the front (1) and side (2) planes of the model's head.*

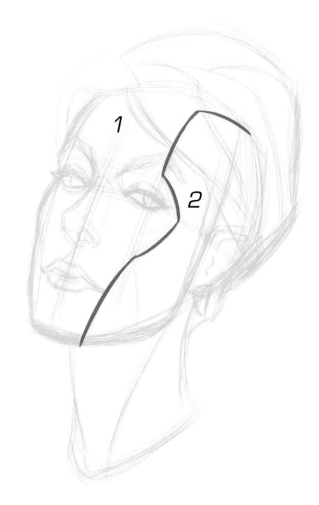

*I relate the arm to a box Form (1) to find its **Turning Edge**.*

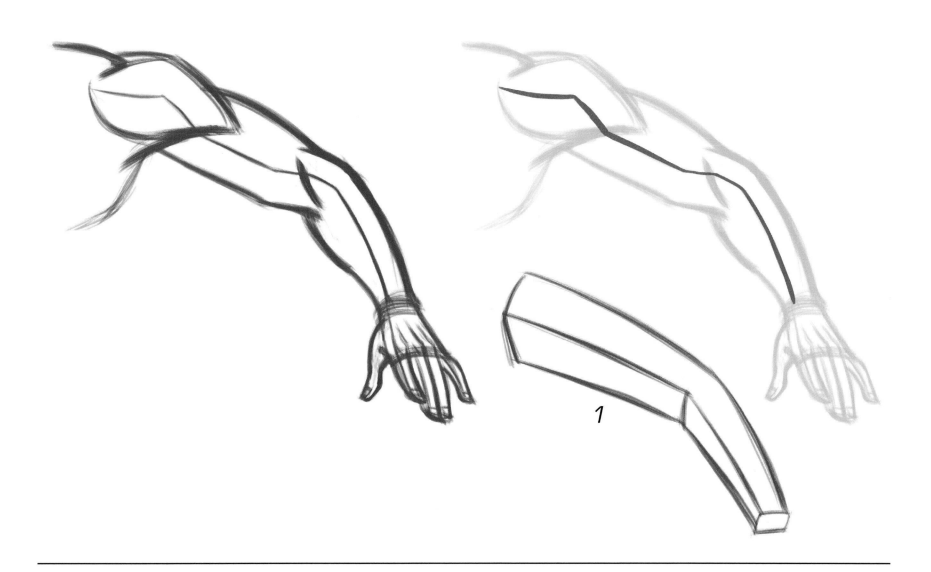

1

*I draw the **Turning Edges** of the lower arm and hand to build the details of the anatomy on top.*

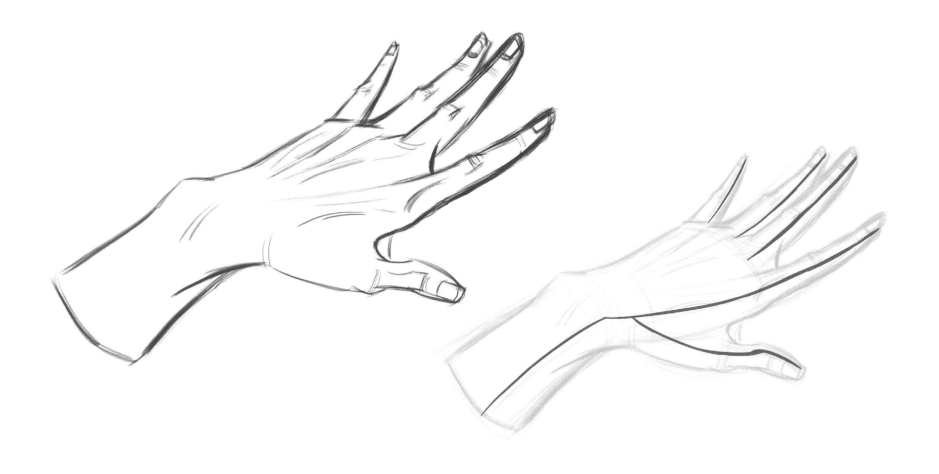

*Watch the **Turning Edges** of the arm and hand. They help you get the Structure right even for complex hand gestures.*

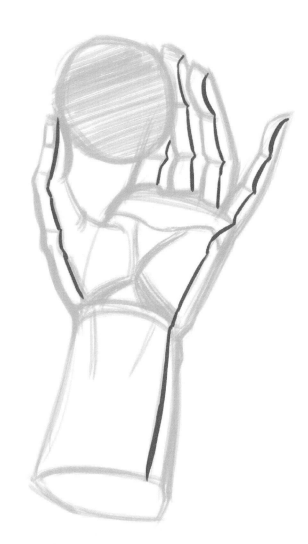

The *Turning Edge* of the legs helps you show their planes.

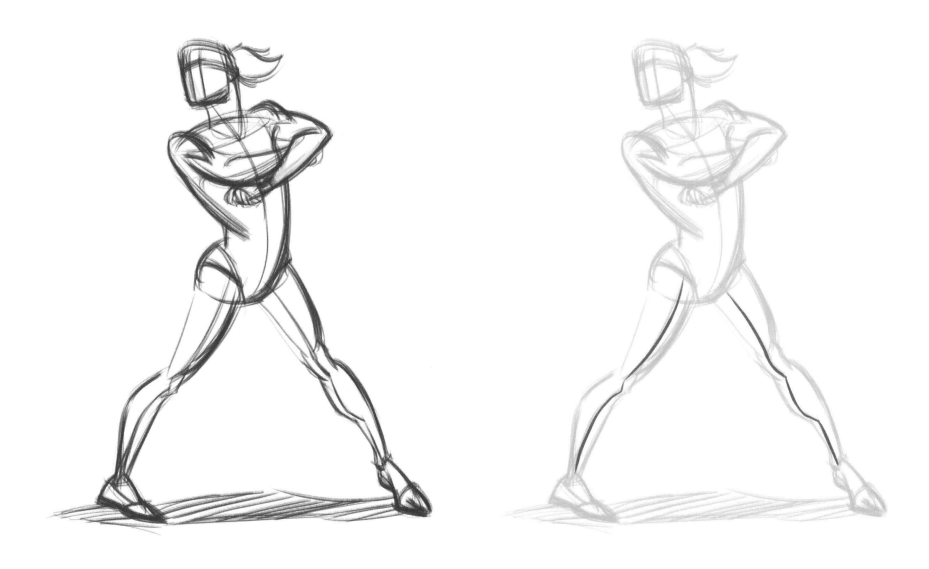

*Also look for the **Turning Edge** at the back of the leg (1).*

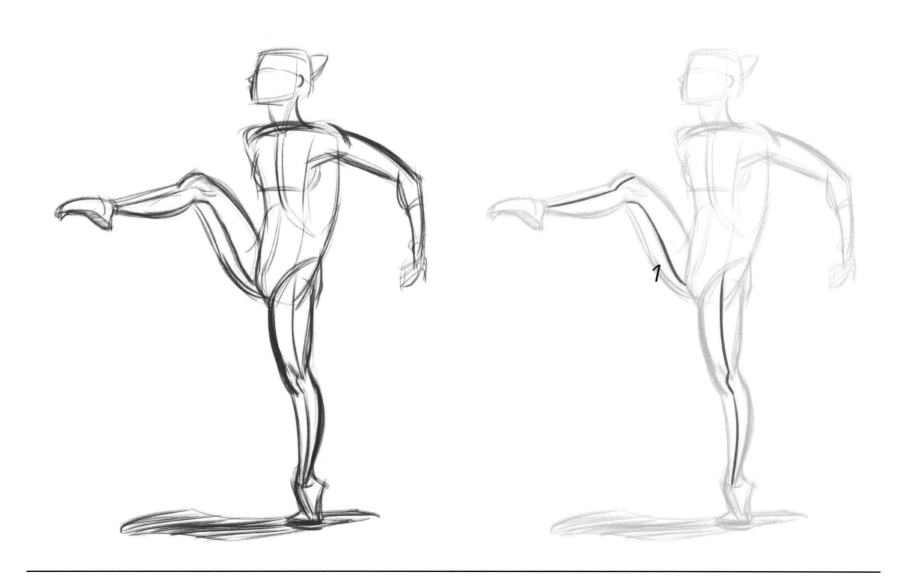

*When you draw the foot, remember to observe how the toes **fit** into its Structure. Also make sure you follow the **Turning Edge** along all parts of the body.*

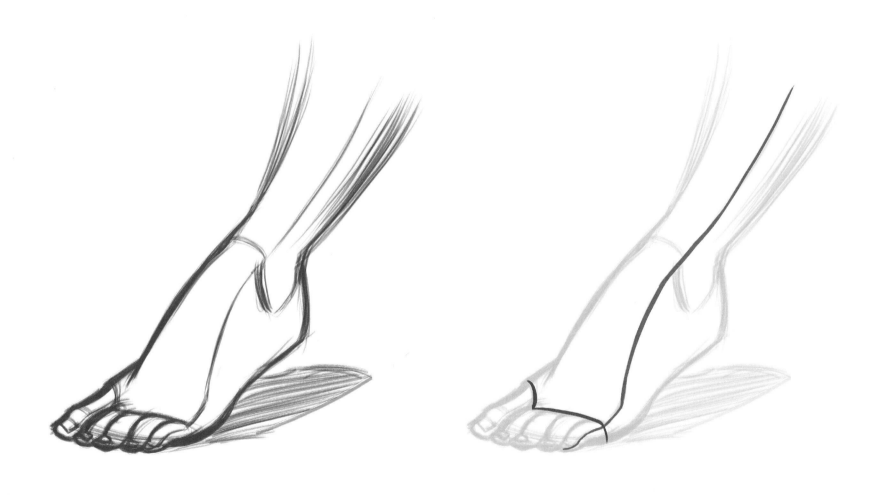

THE CENTERLINE

*The **Centerline** of a Form is another visual tool to help you define Structure.*

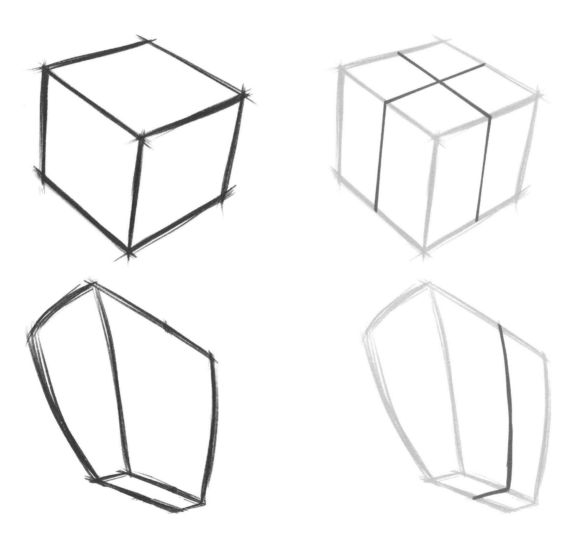

Keep track of anatomical moments, such as the pit of the neck (1) and the sternum (2), that land on the figure's **Centerline**. These are called **Natural Centers**.

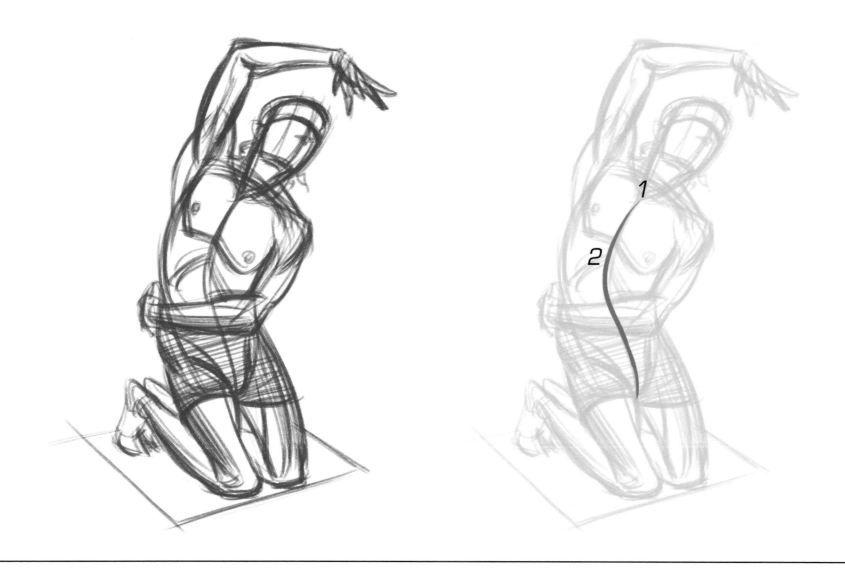

I look for the **Natural Centers** at the back and front of this gymnast's torso to help me understand its twist.

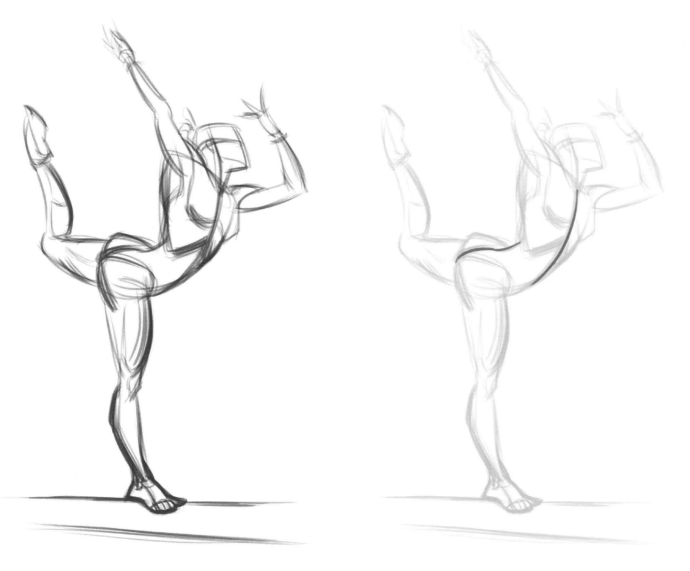

Combine the back's **Natural Center**, in this case the spine, and its **Turning Edge** to get a clearer understanding of the back's Form.

The **Natural Centers** and **Turning Edges** of the athlete's torso and head assist me in defining their Forms.

Use the **Natural Center** and **Turning Edges** of the head to establish a solid structure, and then build the features on top.

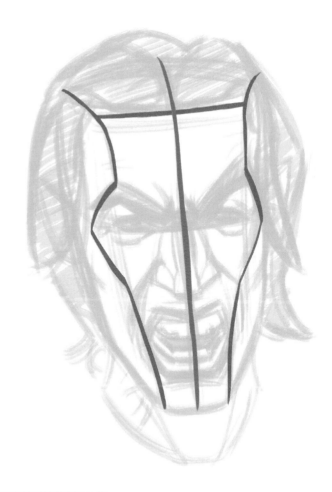

The knee is a good **Natural Center** to keep track of when you draw the leg in front view. In a back view, look for the **Centerline** of the hamstrings and calf muscle.

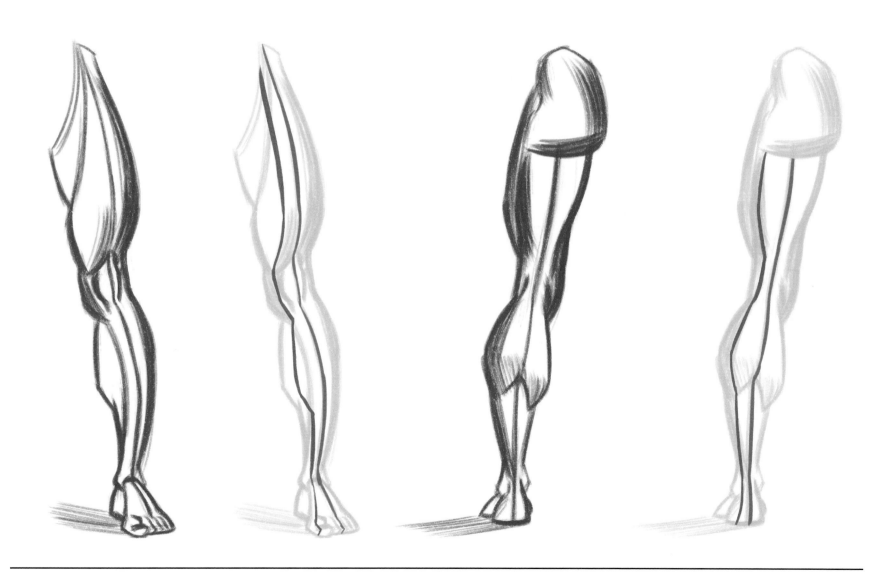

*Observe the **Centerline** and **Turning Edge** of the arm in front view. The **Centerline** runs from the biceps all the way to the middle finger. Notice how the **Centerline** and **Turning Edge** rotate with the lower arm (1).*

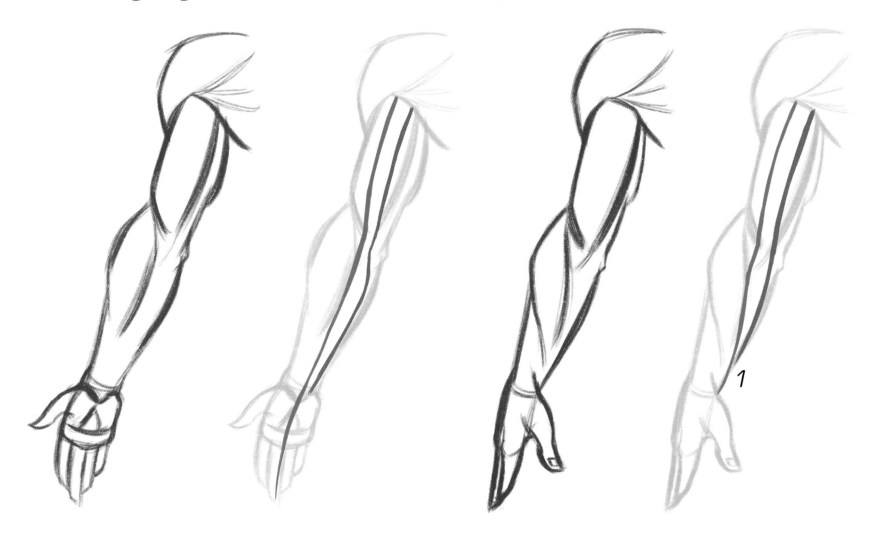

1

*Watch the **Centerline** and **Turning Edges** of the arm in back view. Use the elbow as a **Natural Center**.*

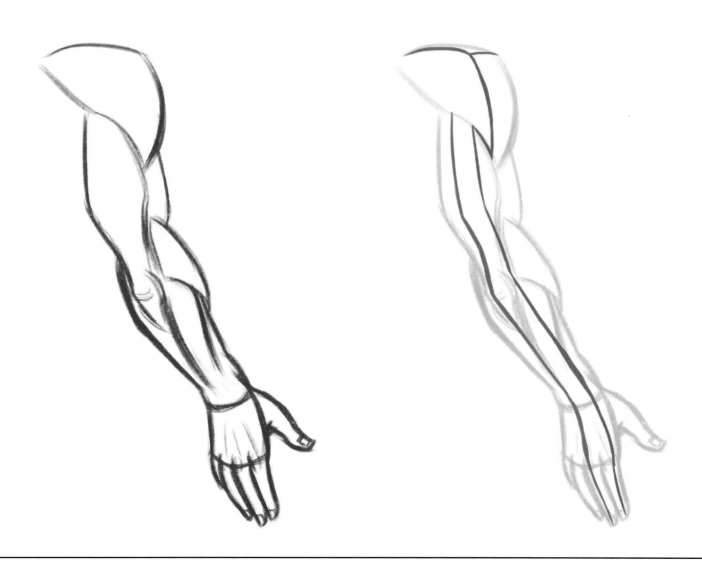

WRAPPING LINES

*Combine **Rhythm** with **Wrapping Lines** to show how FORCE travels in three-dimensional space.*

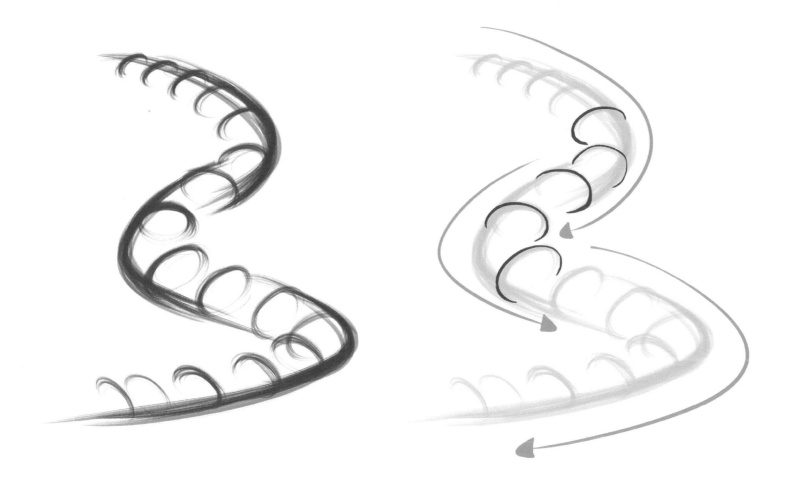

*The **Wrapping Line** on the top of the model's torso is the main one I focus on. It helps me draw the neck and arms in their proper place.*

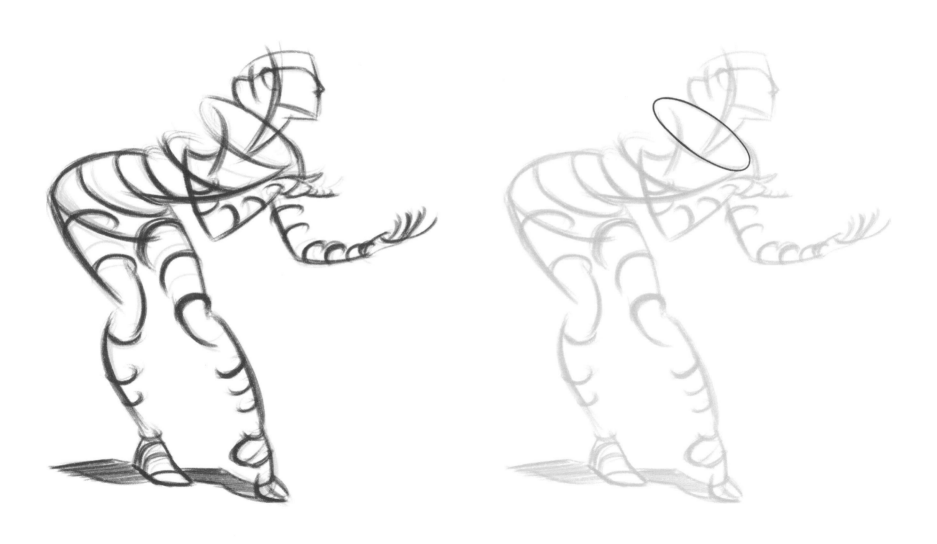

The **Wrapping Lines** on the model's rib cage help me show how it recedes in space.

Here, I draw **Wrapping Lines** on the model's whole body to help me understand his orientation in three-dimensional space.

*I draw the **Wrapping Lines** on the athlete's body parts to help me understand their different orientations in three-dimensional space.*

Notice how the bottom of the model's pectoralis **wraps around** the rib cage. This shows that it goes away from us in space. If the curves are **reversed**, the clarity of the rib cage's Form is lost. Use Wrapping Lines that describe the Forms.

FORCE SURFACE LINES

Wrapping Lines are perpendicular to the Form (1) and show the Form's roundness. *FORCE Surface Lines* that are parallel to the Form (2) create a sense of speed and movement. *FORCE Surface Lines* that are in-between 1 and 2 have a good balance of roundness and movement (3).

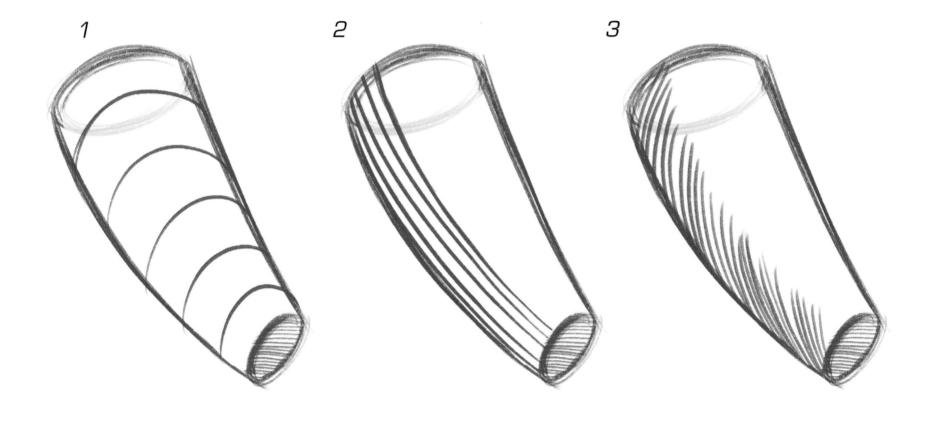

1   *2*   *3*

Always use **FORCE Surface Lines** that adhere to the surface of the Form you're drawing (1). Avoid surface lines that do not explain the Form's surface (2).

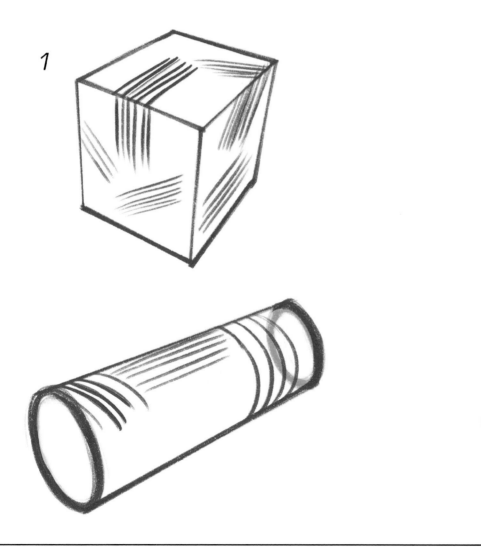

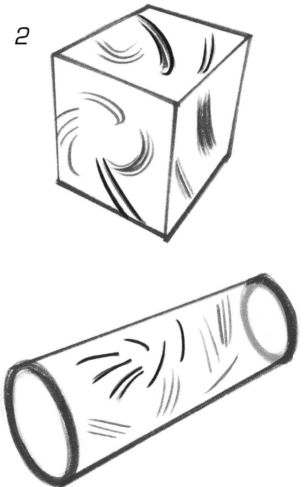

*To develop your skill with **FORCE Surface Lines**, use them to cover as much of the figure's body as possible at the start. Don't be afraid of making mistakes. With practice you'll quickly learn what you should and shouldn't do.*

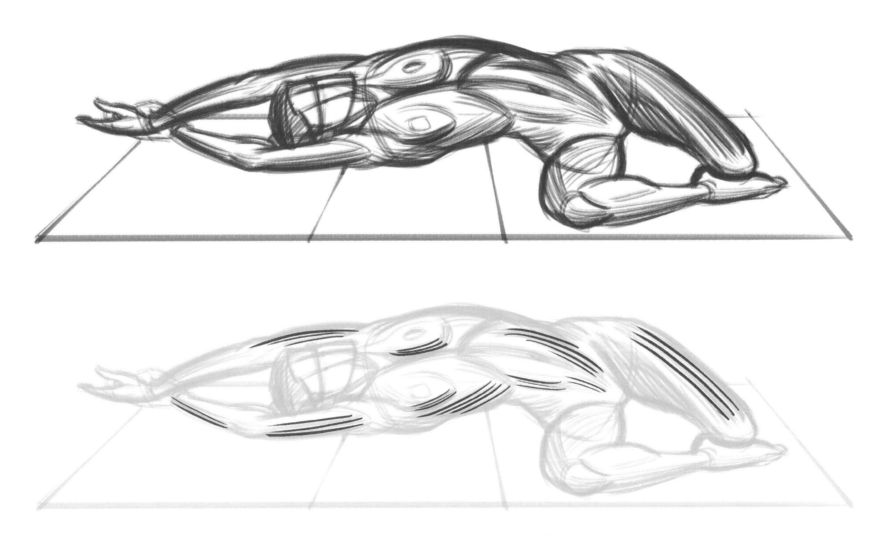

Use **FORCE Surface Lines** to describe the big Forms first. Don't get caught up drawing smaller Forms that don't contribute to the big picture.

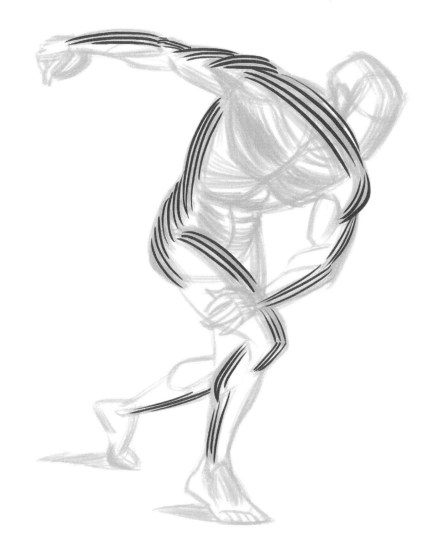

There is a great amount of stretch in this athlete's body as she shoots herself into space. The **FORCE Surface Lines** help me communicate the stretch.

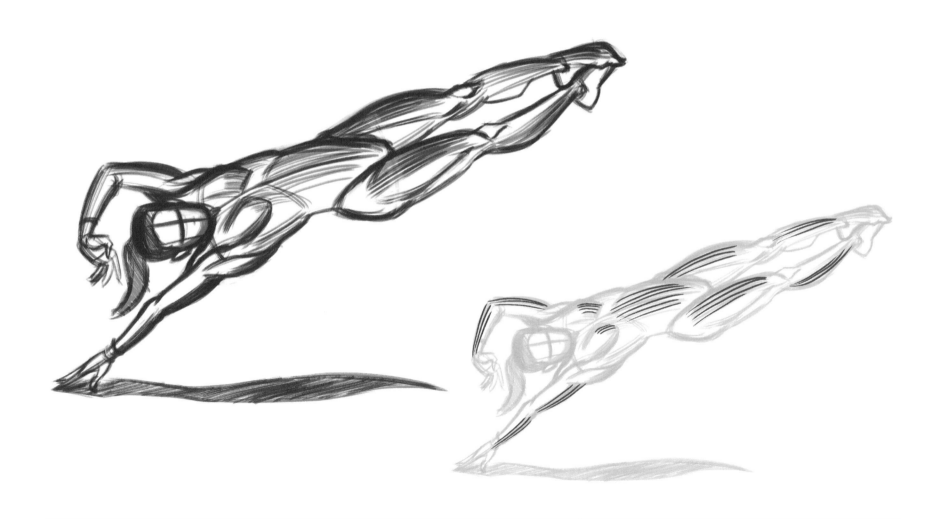

Here, I use darker Directional FORCE Lines at the bottom of the Atlas Stone to emphasize its **weight**. The **FORCE Surface Lines** help me define the Forms of the figure.

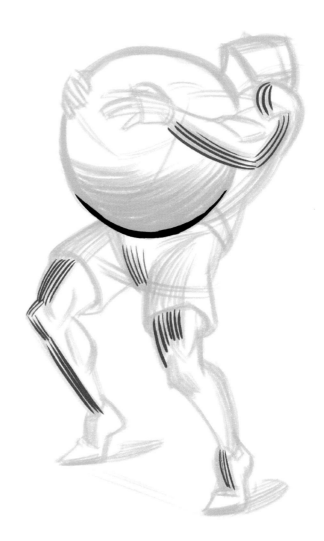

*I like the stretch in this dancer's right pectoralis and arm. I use **FORCE Surface Lines** to emphasize this.*

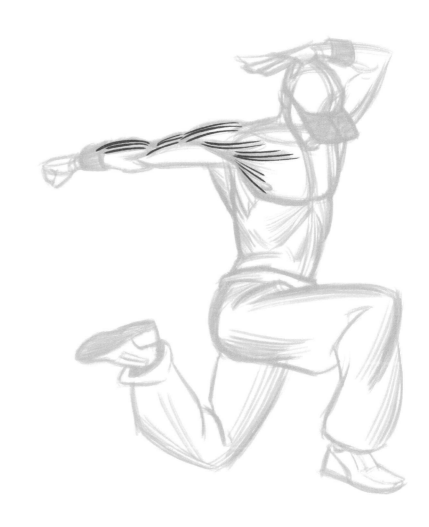

*I use **FORCE Surface Lines** to help me drive FORCE across the martial artist's torso and show its twist.*

To use **FORCE Surface Lines** effectively, act as if you're sculpting the figure. Instead of clay, you use the FORCE Line. Imagine that your pencil's tip is on the figure's body, and that you caress its Forms with every stroke. What does the Form's surface feel like? Draw that.

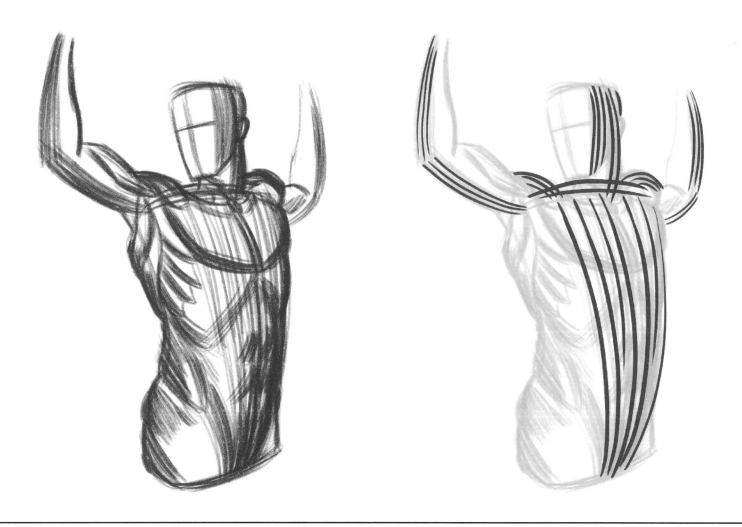

Once you understand the big Forms, use **FORCE Surface Lines** to sculpt the smaller ones.

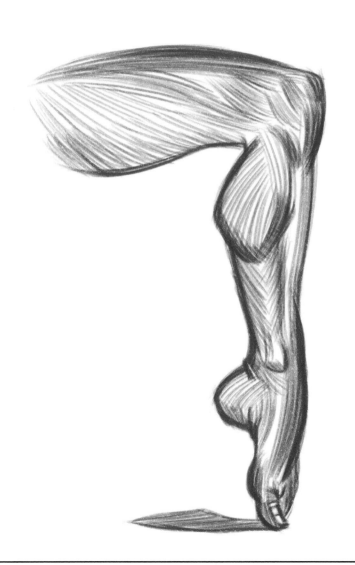
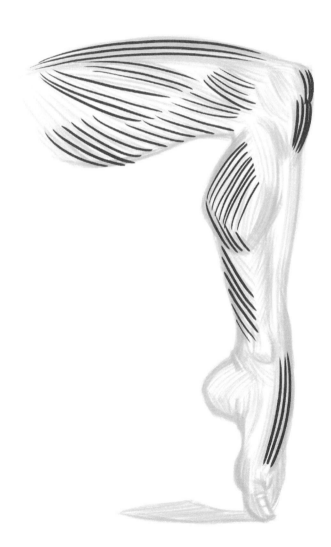

FORCE Surface Lines *help me show the Forms and direction of movement of this body builder's arm.*

Observe how the **FORCE Surface Lines** end at the **Turning Edge** of the upper arm and shoulder. This clearly defines their back and side planes.

*This martial artist's leaning action has a clear Leading Edge. The **FORCE Surface Lines** on his upper torso help accentuate the direction of movement.*

Draw **FORCE Surface Lines** in the direction of the body's *Rhythms*. This enhances the sense of speed and movement in your drawing.

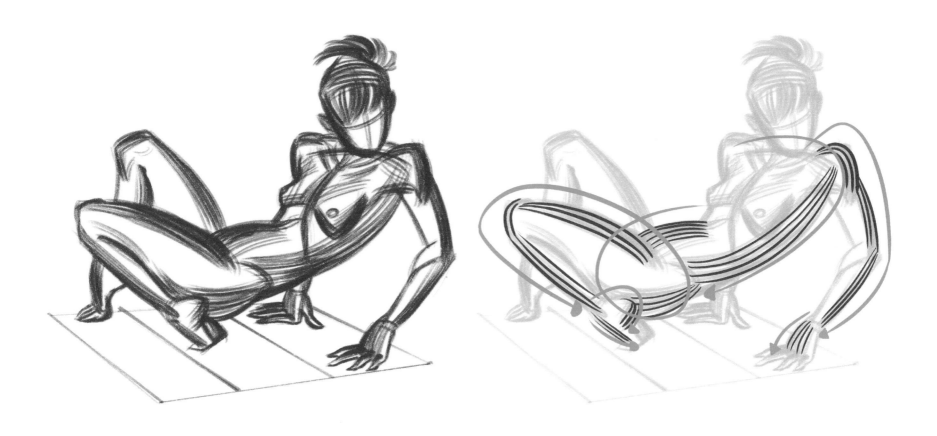

*I use **FORCE Surface Lines** to sculpt the model's Forms and show the different directions of movement.*

*I like the **Rhythm** between the model's torso and left arm in this stretching action. Notice how I use **FORCE Surface Lines** to show the direction of movement and describe Form.*

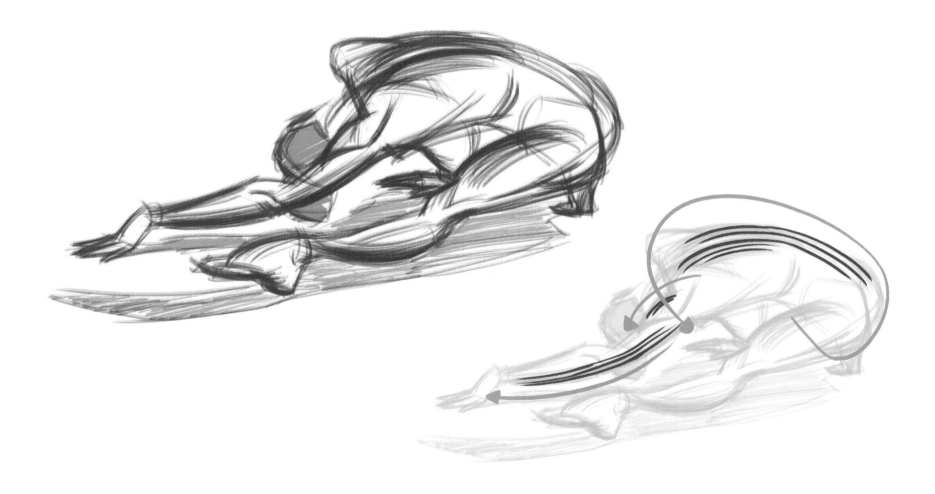

*Check how I draw **FORCE Surface Lines** to flow with the **Rhythms** of the martial artist's legs. This gives the legs a sense of speed.*

*Observe how the **FORCE Surface Lines** show the **C-curve** of the gymnast's torso.*

OVERLAP & TANGENTS

Overlap occurs when one line stops as it touches another. This makes it look like one line has gone behind the other. Thus, *Overlap* creates a sense of depth. A *Tangent* occurs when two lines meet. This creates a sense of flatness, because neither line occupies dominance in space.

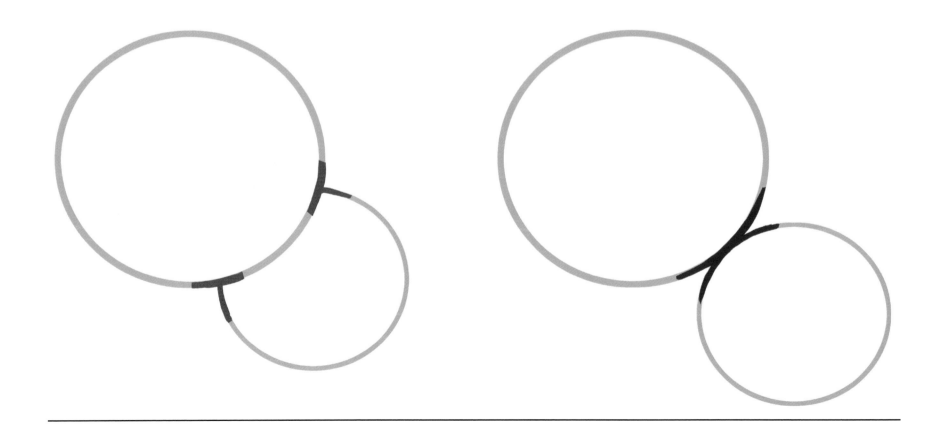

Overlap establishes spatial order in a drawing. Below, we can see that shape 1 is closest to us and shape 5 is farthest away. Since the intersections create a *"T"* *Overlap*, this is also called the "T" rule.

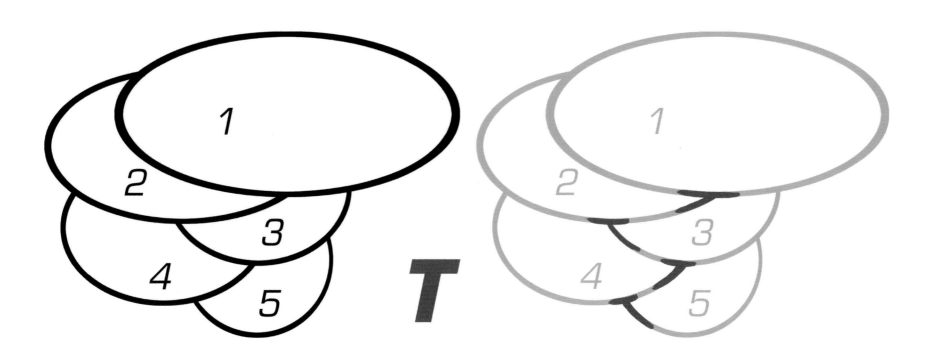

*Check how the model's arms **Overlap** her back. This tells us that the arms are in front.*

Notice the **Overlaps** in this gymnast's left arm. They clarify the spatial order of the arm muscles. **Lack of Overlaps** will flatten the arm.

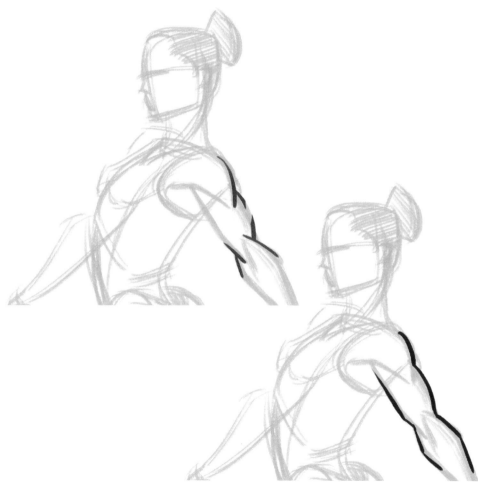

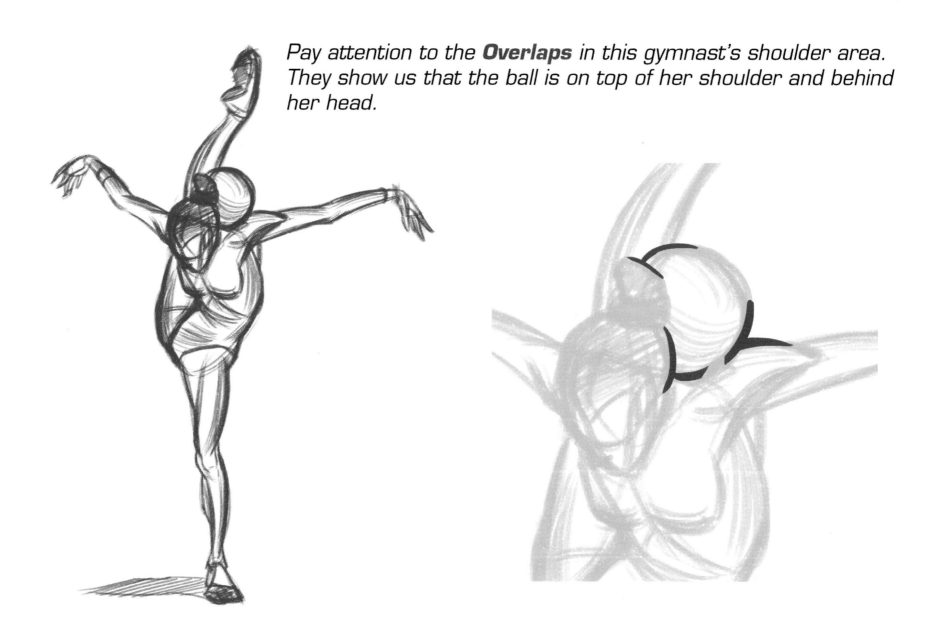

Pay attention to the **Overlaps** in this gymnast's shoulder area. They show us that the ball is on top of her shoulder and behind her head.

One of the major **Overlaps** here is between the martial artist's right shoulder and his head. The **Overlap** between his right elbow, abdomen and left arm shows us that this arm is farther in space.

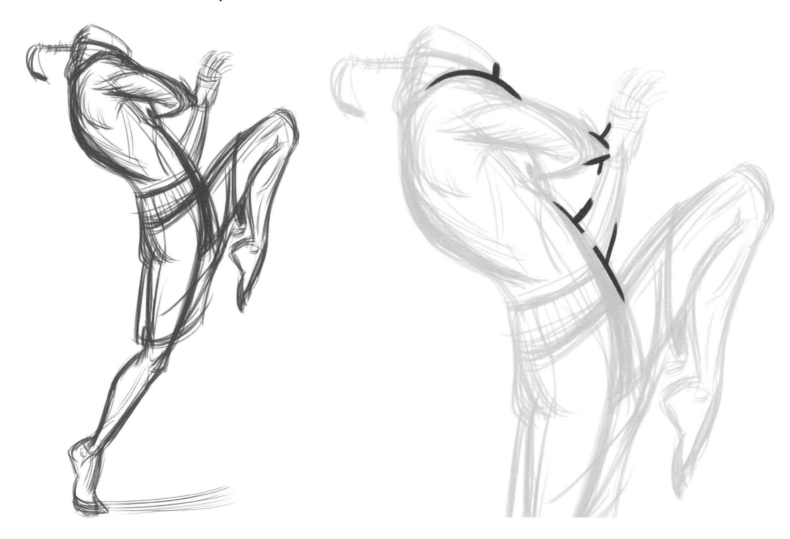

*The clearest **Overlaps** here are the model's face moving in front of her shoulder, her rib cage sticking out in front of her left arm and right hip and her right thigh going in front of the left one. These create a sense of depth.*

Check all the important **Overlaps** in the drawings below. They create clear spatial order in this complex pose.

Chapter 3
FORCE Shape

STRAIGHT TO CURVE DESIGN

*The first row below shows examples of symmetrical or **UnFORCEful Shapes**. Avoid these in your drawings. The second row shows asymmetrical or **FORCEful Shapes**. These give your drawing a sense of energy and movement.*

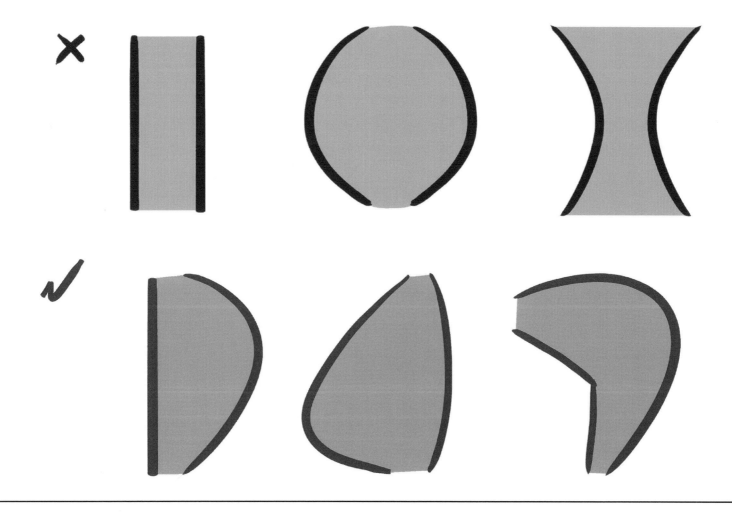

*The most basic **FORCE Shape** consists of a straight line and a curved line. The curve creates a sense of energy and movement. The **straight** creates a sense of Structure.*

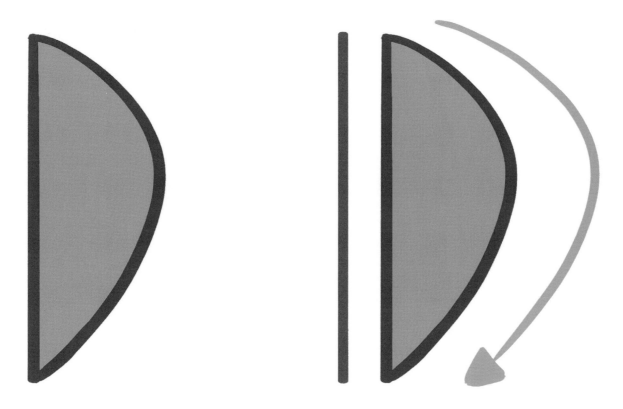

You can draw a **_lesser curve_** on the straight side to make the **FORCE Shape** more organic. Just make sure it doesn't **mirror** the curved side.

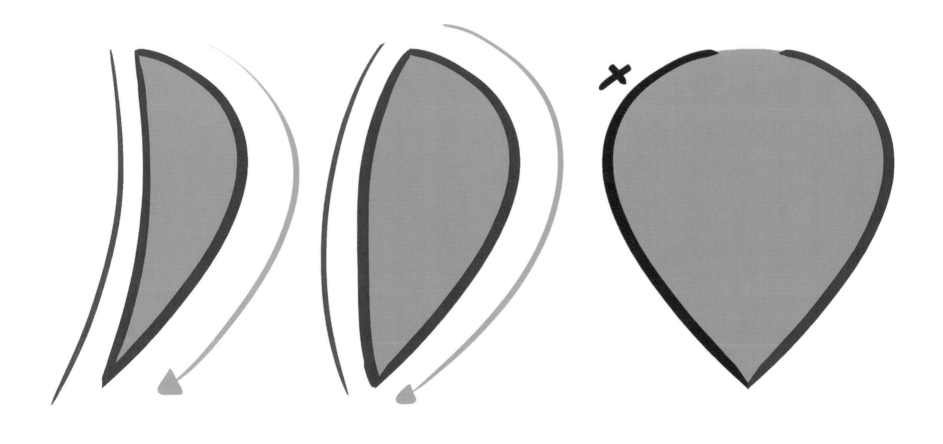

Practice drawing the basic **FORCE Shape** to become familiar with it. Play with the direction and amount of **Applied FORCE** on the curve.

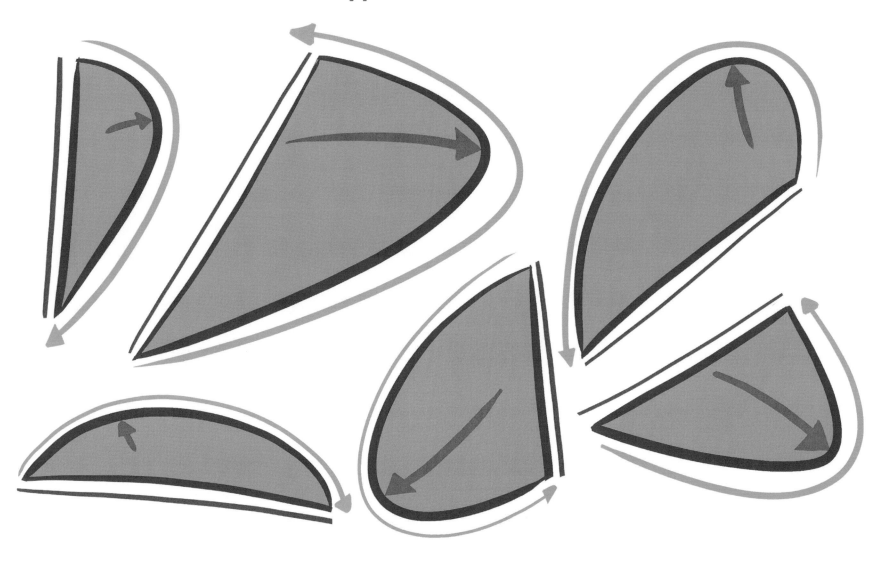

Here are more examples of **FORCE Shapes**. Consider the massive variety in which the rules can be applied. The key is to make the Shapes asymmetrical. Draw some of your own to practice.

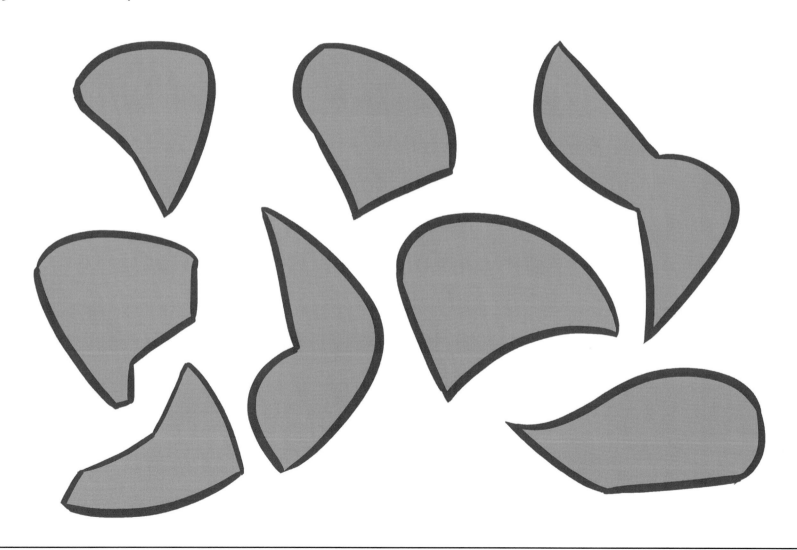

*The figure's biggest Shape is its **Silhouette**. This is the filled-in Shape created by the figure's outline. The Silhouette is made of **FORCE Shapes** (1, 2 and 3).*

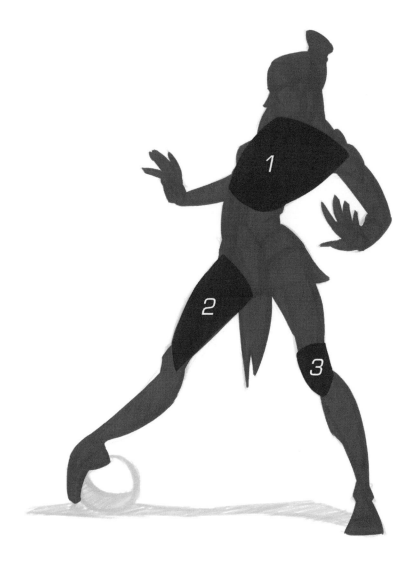

A good **Silhouette** makes the action an easy rea . Remember that the figure's **FORCE Shapes** (1, 2 and 3) create the Silhouette.

*I look at the **Negative Shapes** for placement and to create a clear **Silhouette** while I draw this martial artist.*

*I use **FORCE Shapes** to capture this complex action and look at the **Negative Shapes** to help me with proportions and placement.*

*Observe the strong **FORCE Shape** created by this gymnast's upper torso. The **Negative Shapes** help me with proportion and placement.*

*The rib cage of this dancer has a clear **FORCE Shape**. Notice the **straight** and curve.*

*I like the energy and fluidity of this action. Observe the clear **FORCE Shape** of the figure's rib cage.*

Look at the **FORCE Shape** of this model's midsection. It's pushed out by a strong *Applied FORCE*.

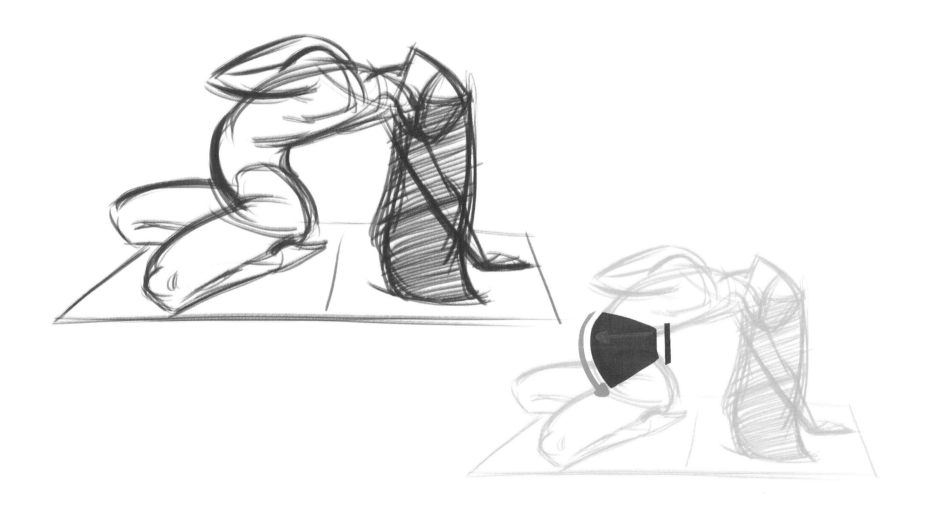

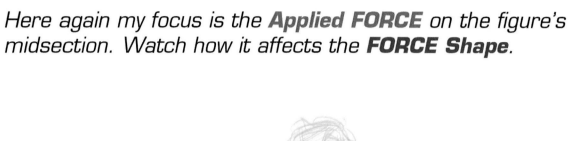

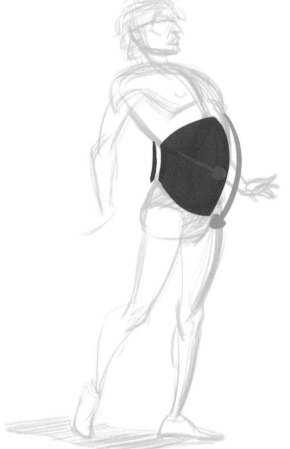

Here again my focus is the **Applied FORCE** on the figure's midsection. Watch how it affects the **FORCE Shape**.

*Notice the **FORCE Shape** of this model's pelvis and how it's affected by the **Applied FORCE**.*

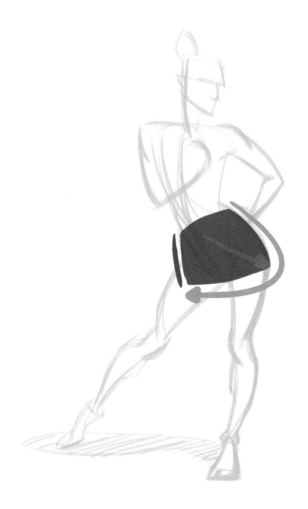

Watch the **FORCE Shape** of this model's pelvis and how it relates to the **Directional** and **Applied FORCEs**.

A

B

C

D

01

Here are the first four frames of a motion study from reference using **FORCE Shapes**. Notice the Leading Edge of the Shape in each frame of action.

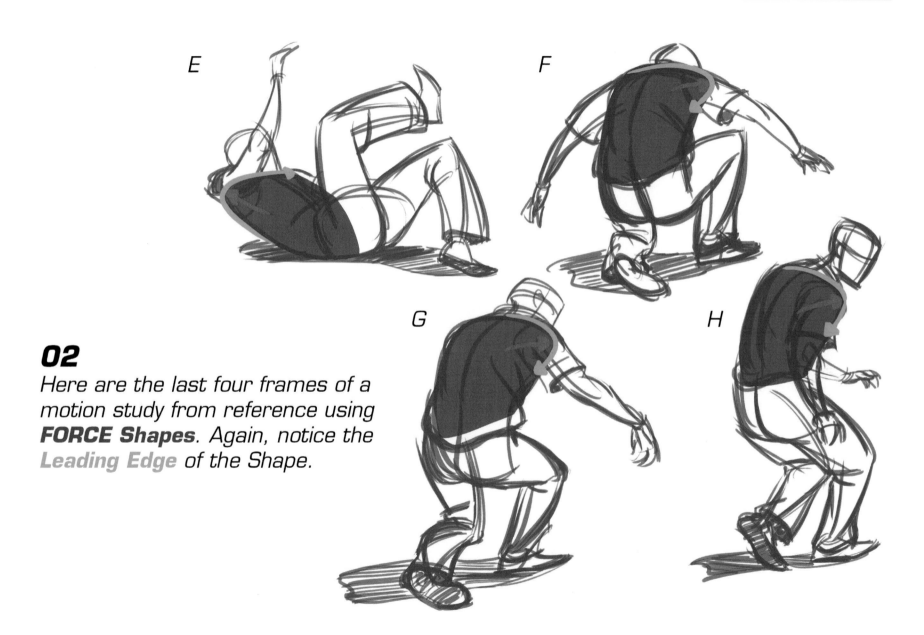

E

F

G

H

02

Here are the last four frames of a motion study from reference using **FORCE Shapes**. Again, notice the **Leading Edge** of the Shape.

See how the **FORCE Shapes** of the model's rib cage (1), midsection (2) and pelvis (3) work with the torso's *Directional FORCE* in the drawing below.

The **Directional FORCE** of the model's bending torso is a clear C-curve. I use this as a basis to draw the torso's three **FORCE Shapes**.

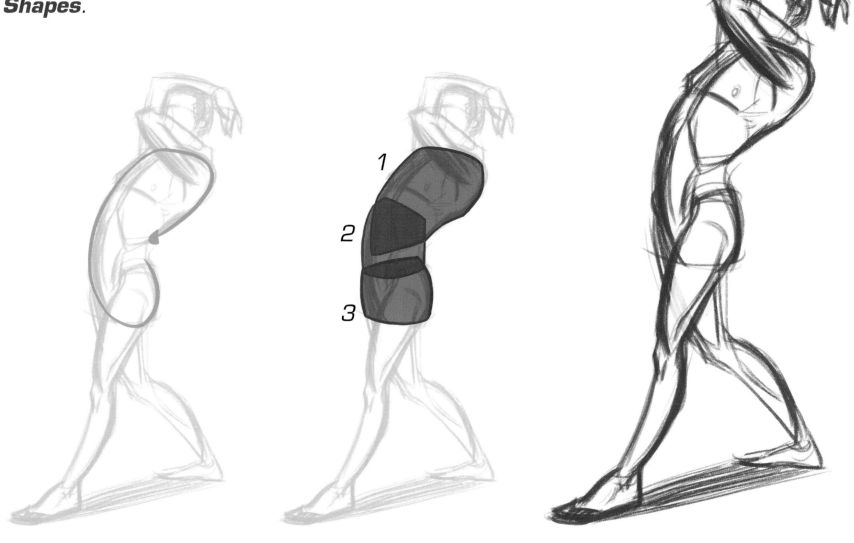

Notice the strong **Applied FORCE** on the dancer's hip. It drags the **FORCE Shapes** of her **R**ib cage, **A**bdomen and **P**elvis to the left.

Next, we combine the **FORCE Shapes** *of the rib cage (1), midsection (2) and pelvis (3) into one big* **FORCE Shape** *for the torso. This is the explanation of the famous Bean (A) and Flour Sack (B) Shapes used in animation.*

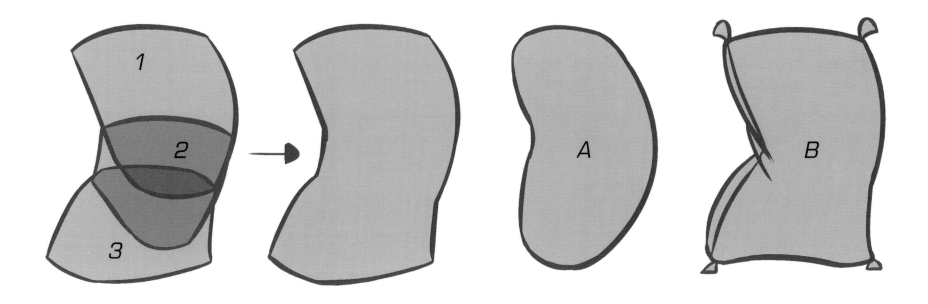

*Following the previous page, I combine the sumo wrestler's rib cage, midsection and pelvis into one **FORCE Shape**. Notice the **Directional** and **Applied FORCEs**.*

I enjoy drawing this gymnast's thrusting head and torso. Watch the torso's **FORCE Shape** *and how it relates to the* **C-curve***.*

*I visualize the model's head as a **FORCE Shape**.
Watch the Directional FORCE and the **straights**.*

Look for the simple **FORCE Shape** of the head and neck and how it connects to the torso.

Here's another example of how I visualize the head and neck as one **FORCE Shape**.

FORCE SHAPE & RHYTHM

I look for the **Rhythm** *between this soccer player's torso, head and neck first. Then I draw their* **FORCE Shapes***.*

Observe the **FORCE Shapes** *of the model's torso, head and neck relative to their* *Rhythms.*

*Look for the simple **FORCE Shapes** of the upper and lower arms before you add any anatomical details. The details won't help if the arms don't work on an abstract level.*

*I use **FORCE Shapes** to draw this athlete's slender and elegant physique.*

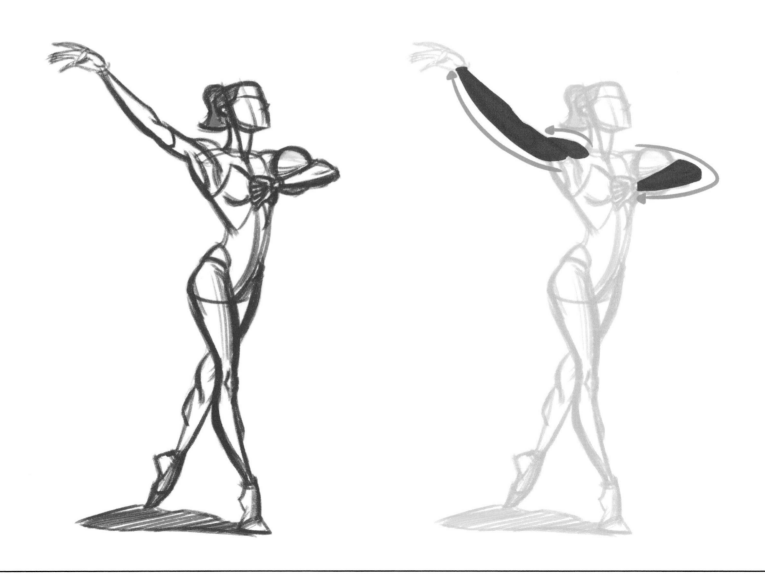

*Notice how the **Directional FORCEs** of the ice skater's arms hold her left leg in place. I use simple **FORCE Shapes** to draw them.*

*Look at the Directional FORCEs and **FORCE Shapes** of this capoeira fighter's arms.*

When you draw hands, look for the **Rhythms** and the **FORCE Shapes**, just like when you draw the body.

*Here, I visualize all four fingers as one **FORCE Shape** to help me draw how they work together.*

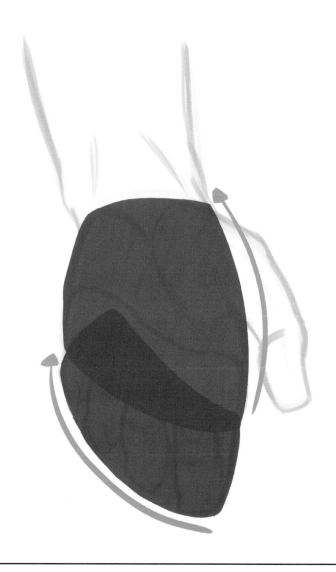

*It helps to group the fingers into **FORCE Shapes** to get the big picture of their action.*

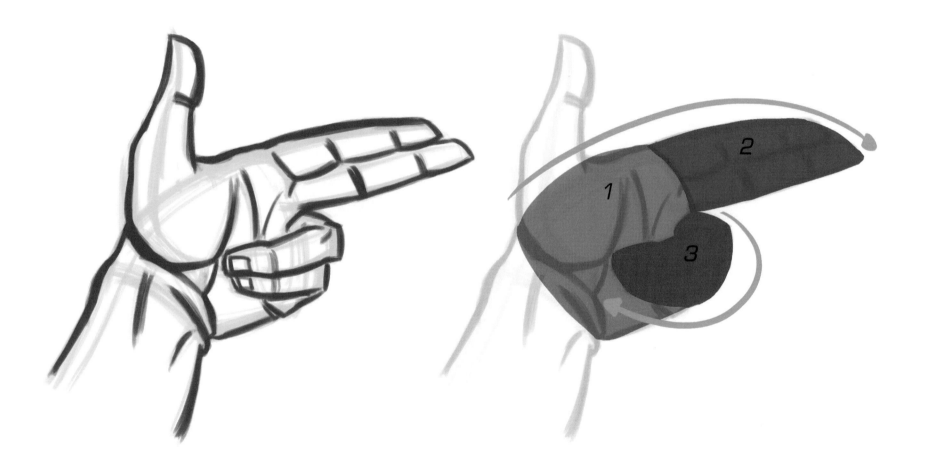

The **FORCE Shapes** *of the fingers resemble the blade of a butter knife (1) during this action.*

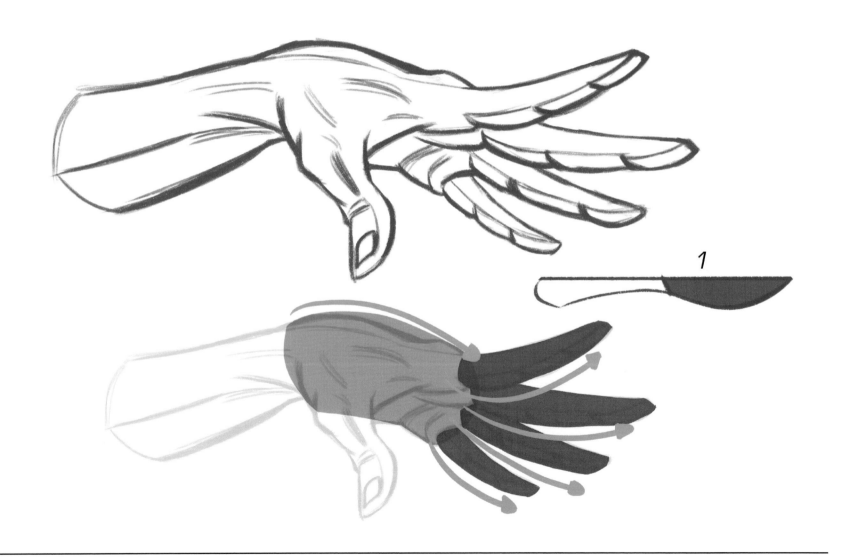

*Make sure the thighs are **FORCE Shapes**. Watch out for **symmetrical Shapes**.*

*The **Rhythms** and **FORCE Shapes** show how the volleyball player's legs work during this action.*

Watch the **FORCE Shapes** of the dancer's legs, and how they have the same *Rhythms*.

This is a three-minute drawing using **FORCE Shapes**. The **Rhythms** of the model's right leg (A) show that it works different than her left leg (B) during this action.

*Remember that **FORCE comes first**. The legs' **Rhythms** give you the basis to design its **FORCE Shapes**.*

Look at the **FORCE Shapes** and different *Rhythms* of the figure's legs. Her right leg has one *Directional FORCE* while her left leg has three.

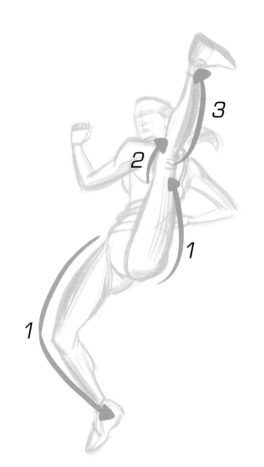

Here, I move from the **FORCE Shapes** of the leg into the foot. Notice the *Rhythms*.

*I like how the toes squash against the floor during the foot's action. Notice the clear **FORCE Shapes**.*

Watch the **Rhythms** *of the lower leg and foot during this action. The ankle bones are like a* **wrench** *that grasps the* **Wedge Shape** *of the foot.*

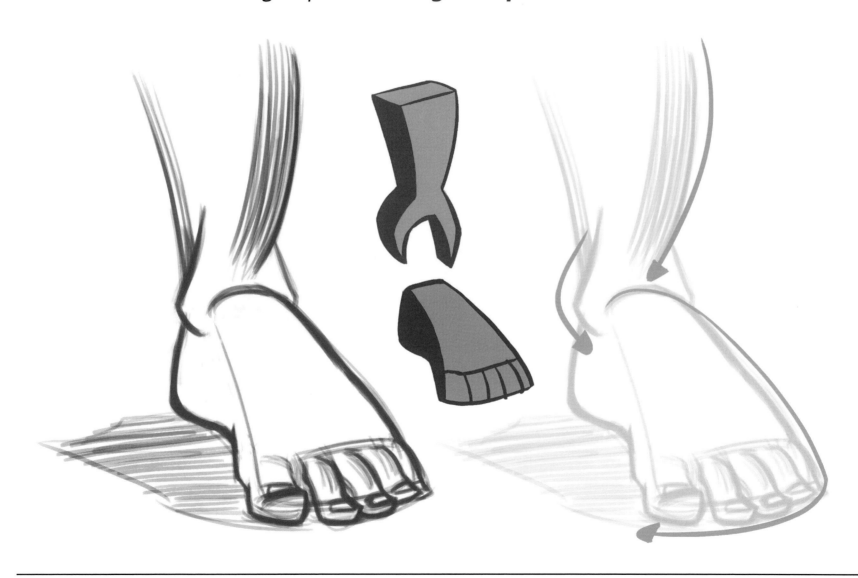

FORCE SHAPE & FORM

*The first way to fill a **FORCE Shape** with Form is to draw its **Turning Edges**. The **Turning Edges** help you understand the different planes of the object you're drawing (1,2 and 1,2,3).*

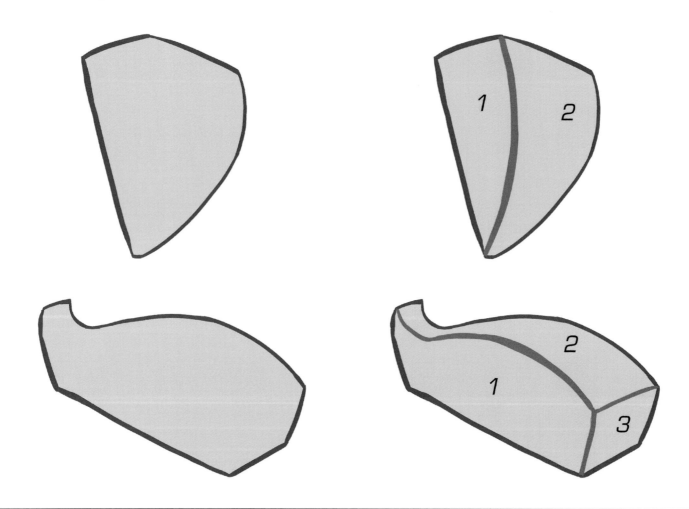

I like the bending torso of this ice skater. I draw the rib cage's **FORCE Shape** *and use its* **Turning Edge** *to fill the Shape with Form. This helps me attach the head and neck.*

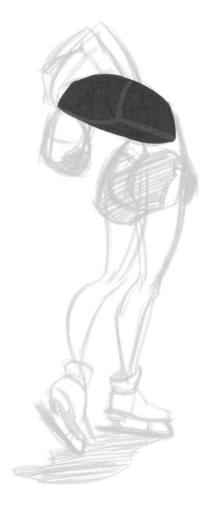

*Notice how I fill the **FORCE Shape** of this dancer's upper torso with Form using its **Turning Edge**. This helps me properly attach her neck, head and arms.*

Here's another example in which I draw the **Turning Edge** to fill the torso's **FORCE Shape** with Form.

*First I draw the **FORCE Shape** of the gymnast's torso. Then I visualize its **Turning Edge** to help me draw the tilt of her pelvis.*

First I find the **FORCE Shapes** of this rugby player's legs to understand how they work. Then I draw their *Turning Edges*.

*I use **FORCE Shapes** to capture the great sense of movement and fluidity of this action. Watch the **FORCE Shapes** and Turning Edges of the model's legs.*

This action has a nice sense of anticipation before the dunk. Watch the simple **FORCE Shapes** and **Turning Edges** of the player's right arm.

*Observe how I fill the **FORCE Shapes** of the lower arm and palm with Form by drawing their **Turning Edges**.*

*I keep the **Turning Edges** of the hand's palm in mind when I draw its **FORCE Shape**. This gives me a basis to attach the fingers.*

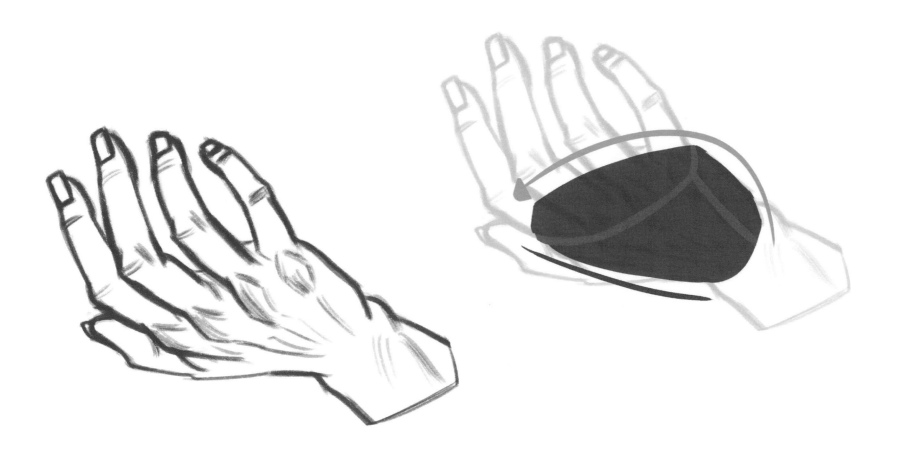

After I draw the **FORCE Shapes** *of the fingers, I draw their* **Turning Edge**
to fill them with Form.

*I draw the **FORCE Shapes** of the fingers first, and then draw their **Turning Edges** to add a sense of Form.*

Use *Wrapping Lines* to fill the **FORCE Shapes** with Form.

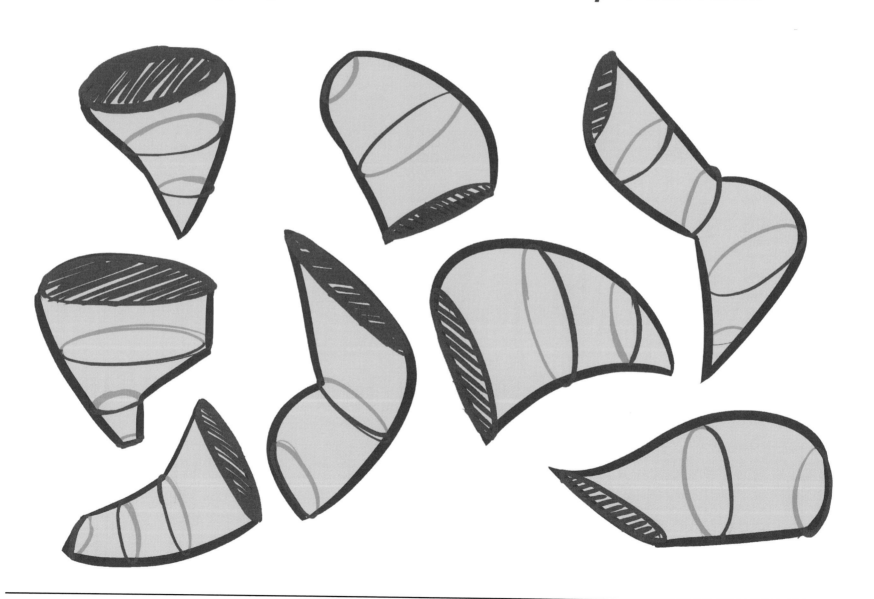

This is a good exercise to prepare you to use **FORCE Shapes** to draw the figure. First, draw some Directional FORCEs (1). Then add a straight (or lesser curve) at the opposite of each Directional FORCE (2). And finally, use Wrapping Lines to fill the Shapes with Form (3).

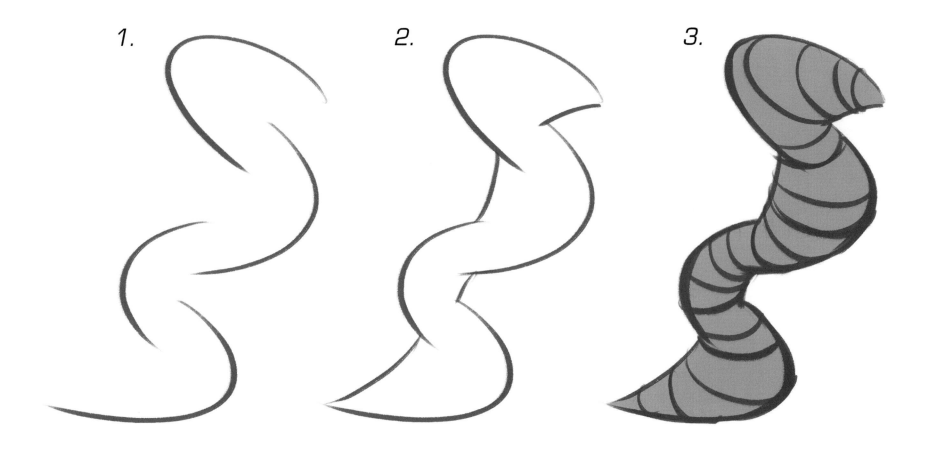

*Here I visualize **Wrapping Lines** on the **FORCE Shape** of the torso to get a sense of its Form.*

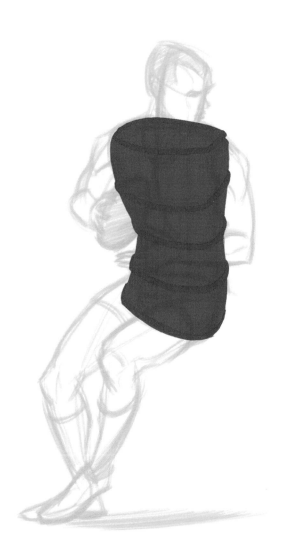

I use **FORCE Shapes** *to draw this hockey player and visualize* **Wrapping Lines** *on the Shapes to get a sense of the torso's Form.*

Even though I draw the model's arm with **FORCE Shapes**, I'm aware of its **Wrapping Lines** and its direction in three-dimensional space.

When I draw the **FORCE Shapes** of the rugby player's arms, I'm aware of their **Wrapping Lines**. This helps me depict their foreshortening.

*I draw the **FORCE Shapes** of this athlete's left leg with its **Wrapping Lines** in mind. This helps me understand the leg's direction in three-dimensional space.*

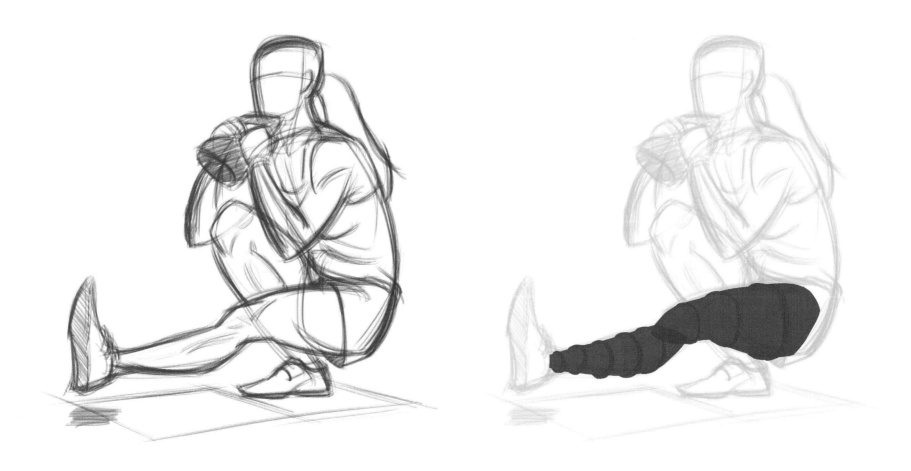

*I focus primarily on the model's legs in this quick drawing. They are key for him to stay balanced. The **Wrapping Lines** of the leg's **FORCE Shapes** show their orientation in three-dimensional space.*

SHAPE SIZE FOR DEPTH

*To push the sense of depth in the drawing, I make the **FORCE Shape** of the model's closer foot bigger than the **FORCE Shape** of the farther foot.*

*Notice the small **FORCE Shape** of the farther foot compared with the **FORCE Shape** of the closer foot. The greater the size difference, the greater the sense of depth.*

*Watch how the size difference between the **FORCE Shapes** of the figure's left and right feet enhances the perception of space in the drawing.*

*I draw the **FORCE Shape** of the athlete's right hand bigger than his left hand to show that it's closer to us.*

Here, the hand's big **FORCE Shape** in contrast to the smaller **FORCE Shape** of his head shows us which one is closer.

Observe the size variance between the **FORCE Shapes** of the basketball player's hands, head and feet to enhance the sense of space.

Here the larger **FORCE Shapes** of the model's right thigh and upper arm in contrast to their counterparts increase the perception of space.

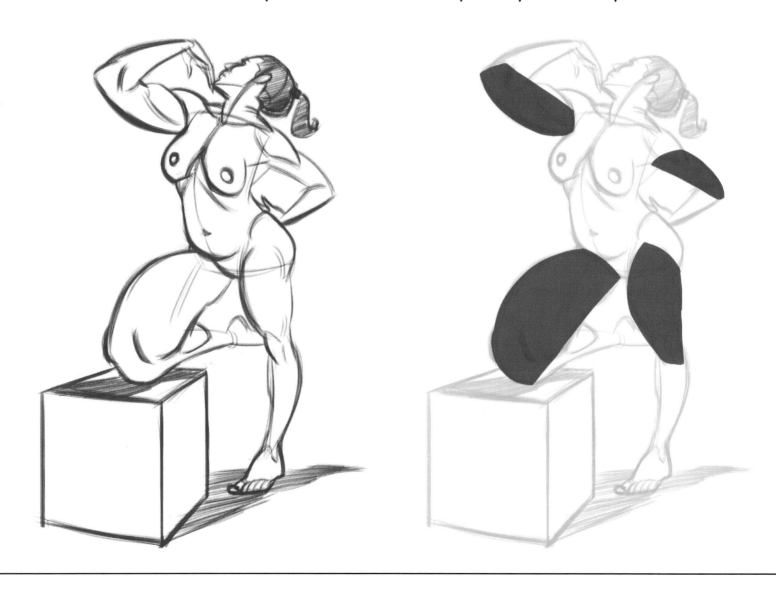

*I enlarge the **FORCE Shapes** of the gymnast's feet relative to the rest of her body to push it back in space.*

REACTION

My reaction to this model is his massive upper body. I make his midsection and pelvis smaller to show this.

Here I react to the athlete's long, slender physique. I add some FORCE Surface Lines to enhance the perception of motion.

I exaggerate the size of the model's muscles to push my opinion about how he's built.

Index